wake up, church!

Opening your eyes to transformational ministry

ED KRUSE
BILL STEADMAN

WAKE-UP, CHURCH!
Opening Your Eyes to Transformational Leadership

Publishing Consultant: Huff Publishing Associates LLC

Cover and Book Design: Marti Naughton

CONGREGATIONS WHO TAUGHT US

PEOPLE WHO PRAYED FOR US

CRITIQUES WE RECEIVED

FRIENDS AND FAMILY WHO SUPPORTED US

LACKING WISDOM WE TAKE RESPONSIBILITY

VALUE FOR WHICH WE PRAISE GOD

CONTENTS

INTRODUCTION

Billy Graham said, "The church is a sleeping giant. If that giant ever wakes up, look out."[1] This inspired us authors—Ed Kruse, a Lutheran, and Bill Steadman of The United Church of Canada. We wondered, "Was Graham intending to single out a specific denomination? Could he have called any denomination a sleeping giant?" Is there an inspiring application of this message to the church today?

We want to begin by shifting away from using the biblical word "church" in fuzzy ways, and shift toward using the term to express faith relationships and faith practices. Our faith relationships and faith practices are the embodiment of our identity and purpose as part of God's church. In this sense, we can say "our congregation" and we can speak of being intimately connected to "the body of Christ." We have been given faith relationships and faith practices and when we connect these faith relationships with our identity and our purpose, we can say so more clearly.

We have an identity and we have a purpose. Our identity is that God created, redeemed, and transformed us to be in relationship with others and with God. Our identity is inseparably connected to our purpose. We want to use the term "wake up" as a metaphor for revitalizing our purpose of being ambassadors for reconciling the world to God through Jesus Christ, the Holy Spirit empowering us to glorify God and build up the body of Christ.

When we clarify the conversation in this way, we access God's transformation. When we clarify our identity and our purpose, we hold to our faith values. We also express our faith relationships toward expanding God's mission on earth. In a phrase, we are committed to congregation renewal.

We want to limit our use of "church" as a synonym for "organized religion" or the "institutional." Using such terms interchangeably makes for

1 Billy Graham, at the U.S. Congress on Evangelism, 1969.

fuzzy communication at best. At worst, such conversations turn accusatory, critical, scapegoating, avoid dealing with our own frustration, or justify our human practice of complaining. The net effect of co-mingling these cultural definitions with biblical understanding is that such conversations distract us from the central conversation about mission, God's mission.

Wake Up, Church! is a call to action. The intent of this book is to refocus the conversation, using the adjective "sleeping" as a metaphor. And the reader can expect the context of the conversation to bluntly suggest that it is time for any congregation that is asleep to wake up.

Billy Graham's comment was specific in reference that "the Lutheran Church is a sleeping giant; and if that giant ever wakes up, look out!" Some who heard him said, "I'm glad he did not include our denomination." Others said, "How do you know he did not intend that meaning? I think the message fits my tribe." We considered the evangelist's statement to be a worthwhile basis for conversation for all denominations. We concluded that his statement could be a fruitful action and an urgent wake-up call to all who share their heritage of proclaiming the good news of Jesus Christ as revealed in God's Word.

Are we sleeping? Have we dozed off? Have we all fallen asleep at the switch? Have we been distracted from our legacy? Have we distorted the good news of Jesus Christ?

Is there still time to wake up to the transformational power of the Holy Spirit? The potential of any fruitful conversation is that it can become a joyful opportunity to act. It can also be serious and urgent. Dare we ask, "Have we hindered others from being reconciled to God through Jesus Christ?"

Does the Institutional Church Need Transforming?

The question for us is, "Is Graham's observation accurate today?" Many criticize organized religion for being more than just asleep at the switch. Mainline traditions acknowledge that they are in danger of being irrelevant. Some think "sleeping" is not harsh enough. They say we have not simply fallen asleep, but have abandoned our theological heritage, leadership development, and missional purpose. Some say that we have ignored Jesus.

Still others accuse these critics of ignoring the many great things the congregation has done to help reconcile the world to God through Jesus Christ by developing educational institutions, hospitals, disaster response organizations, health care agencies, advocacy for children, and seeking justice in the world, including advocating for peace, for just mining and farming activities, for the availability of clean water, and for fair labor practices around the world. That is valid too.

One of the consequences of being asleep at the switch is that we have not become more adept at dealing with our theological differences in a relational way. One writer said, "The greatest heresy of our day is the withholding of our love from people with whom we do not agree on every point."[2]

God has every reason to expect us to deal better with social issues, character defects of our clergy and congregation leaders, and matters of justice. Instead, we worry about protecting ourselves. We have a black eye for the ways we have dealt with sexual misconduct, same-sex marriage, and civic responsibilities. Fractured relationships are tragic, especially in the congregation.

For some, these realities have nullified the faith that is reflected in hope. Has the congregation abandoned God's mission of giving people hope? Are you excited about our invitation to replace criticism and condemnation with the hope that comes from the Holy Spirit? If the congregation is in need of revitalization, one of our purposes must be to grow through sharing God's hope to a seriously discouraged and despairing world.

Wake up, Church! suggests transformational ways to address many factors that have contributed to the demise of organized religion. Our vocabulary has become unclear. Social decline has increased. In spite of its good intentions, the "church" has allowed a values vacuum to infiltrate our society. Some cultural trends have filled that vacuum with sports, leisure, consumerism, and even privacy matters. Sometimes our priorities have simply been surrendered by default. Current research indicates that 53% to 80% of congregation members do not participate in congregation

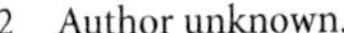

2 Author unknown.

ministries.[3] It bears repeating that congregations have failed to adequately challenge these realities.

An assumption of this book is that congregations can find hope in their faith. God's promises are still sure. The Holy Spirit still provides the wisdom and the energy for transformation. Jesus himself came to share a message of hope in a bleak period of human history. It is up to us to be as resourceful and clear in living God's mission as Jesus was.

The Holy Spirit empowers our faith practices. We can encourage our leaders. It is possible to stop the bloodletting and decline. It is possible to increase participation in congregation ministries. It is possible to re-engage former active participants to serve in their areas of giftedness. Leaders can become receptive. They want to experience God in their lives. We make a mistake if we think we should lower expectations. We often do not trust leaders enough to ask more from them. Councils and congregations can get excited to try creative ideas. Congregation decision-making can become open to listening and can rethink how to expand God's mission. All of this is possible through the Holy Spirit. You can help make it happen.

For example, what might happen if we were to respectfully focus on the neglected group we used to call "inactive members?" What if we were to redefine this audience into a threefold group—the Uninvolved, the Under-involved, and the Uninvited.

If we were to respect the Uninvolved, Under-involved, and Uninvited members, might we expand our understanding? Might we discover that they too are actually gifts of God? Might we discover some future leaders? This audience is intergenerational! It is a giant resource for congregation renewal! Congregations can be renewed by the Holy Spirit working through young adults, youth, and children.

We can address these issues in ways that increase trust and respect within congregations. It will help if we understand some of the principles of transformational leadership. Of course, leaders can learn approaches and strategies that are more effective. Every generation sets out to discover them. What is striking is that transformational leadership principles have the capacity to develop momentum early in the process.

3 Current research by HealthierChurch.org

We might ask how long transformational leadership has been in vogue. Let's put it in perspective.

Is Transformational Leadership a New Idea?

More books have been written about leadership in the last decade than in the past two centuries. This is especially true of transformational leadership. It's interesting that before 1985, there was no mention of transformational leadership. In 2008, however, when we Googled "transformational leadership" in preparation for a presentation, we found a list of 462,000 entries. And a short six months later, the list had grown to 1,570,000.

It is possible that these statistics will one day be interpreted as a passing fancy. It is clear, however, that there is a great deal of interest in what it means to be "transformational." At the same time, this is not to say that current authors are not building on previous approaches to leadership, and some of them clearly date back to New Testament times.

One of today's recognized leaders in transformational approaches is Ron Heifetz, who pioneered some transformational principles under a new heading called adaptive leadership. Michael White described an approach called narrative theory, or narrative therapy that provided transformation in marriages and families. Peter Drucker became a strong advocate for transformation under the banner of servant leadership.

Bernard Bass coined the term "transformational leadership," and courses in Transformational Leadership are now available for college credit.

A key spokesperson for transformation within congregations is Dr. Phyllis Tickle, who has applied transformational leadership to what some call the emerging church. Seminaries are now offering opportunities for future clergy to learn about transformational leadership.

We could make the case that transformational leadership is not a new idea. Jesus' parables clearly reframe traditional principles in new ways. Jesus also reframed the commandments in a transformational way, "You have heard it said...but I say unto you..." Jesus interpreted God's law and summarized it, "A new commandment I give you..." The intended outcome of all of this, of course, was transformational living.

Toward a Definition of Transformational Leadership

Wikipedia, a non-religious entity, defines transformational leadership in a way that speaks to us in the church. Please notice the key words: "*Transformational leadership is an approach that creates valuable and positive change in the followers, with the end goal of developing followers into leaders...It enhances the motivation, morale, and performance...it connects one's sense of identity and self to the mission and the collective identity of the organization.*"

The definition is applicable to our congregation, our country, and our family. The wake-up call applies to us. We seem to be terminally unable to make only good choices. We seem to be terminally passing the buck to others instead of accepting responsibility. We seem to be chronically forgetting to live in God's promises.

Chapter 1 begins with the need to "Clean Up Your Language." Words matter. There is special importance to clarifying what we mean by "church." Chapters 2 through 12 introduce one or more principles of transformational leadership that have the capacity to teach us:

- Holding on and letting go
- Taking on more activities while respecting our limits
- Inviting with transformational hospitality
- Handling our feelings, thoughts, and actions, and those of others
- Re-inventing our vision of hope
- Listening to new ways to live the Gospel
- Simplifying our lives
- Taking our time quickly
- Overcoming roadblocks to transformational leadership
- Praying transformationally

We claim our theme, "Wake Up, Church!" in confidence and hope. God has given us the power to create space for the Holy Spirit to wake up the congregation and transform it. When we get our wake-up call, we can joyfully respond, "Thank you!" Living into God's call to be a follower of Christ is the direction we all need, and we all benefit from regular reminders. What is surprising is that this opportunity is beyond our understanding, and yet is so simple.

I

Cleaning Up Our Language

"Let no evil talk come out of your mouth, but only what is useful for building up... Put away from you all bitterness and wrath and anger and wrangling and slander, together with all malice, and be kind to one another, tenderhearted, forgiving one another, as God in Christ has forgiven you."[1]

Purposeful Communication

We suggest that all communication is out of order that does not enhance any person's God-given dignity. We further suggest that both congregation renewal and transformation of our culture depend greatly on our shifting to redemptive communication. Using language in our congregations that is uplifting, hopeful, and builds community is appropriate for doing the work of God. If our words seek to accomplish none of these goals, we are in a congregation that is laced with profanity.

Perhaps for Christians the worst profanity is not particular four letter words but to say, "I don't care." What can be more profane than to withhold our love from someone? Or worse, to say that we have no interest in their well-being or future? The opposite of love is not hate: it is not caring at all, living a life of complete disinterest in another. Jesus commands us to love one another, not to be disinterested in one another. We show our love not only in caring and communicating, but in how we do that. Among other things, we convey our intent by the tone of voice we use.

1 Ephesians 4:29, 31-32.

Your Words Imply Your Intent

Jesus often broadened the definitions of different terms so as to include the intention of the person. Perhaps we should define profanity as "anything that demeans the other person or lessens the redemptive nature of the relationship."

In that light, does name-calling fall into the category of profanity? Does judgmentally labeling the motives of others qualify as profanity? There has been a lot of discussion about the societal practices of bullying. This can be an extreme example of profanity—using words beyond their wholesome meaning to belittle and defame. Oftentimes bullying is more than verbal; it includes physical attacks and threats, hatred in slogans on buildings, or burning another's possessions as an act of disrupting, even scaring, the other's well-being.

Why are cautions about such judgmental, bullying, and labeling talk important as we think of congregation renewal for the future? For many years the church in North America has had a "bully pulpit." We have presented our views as the only views, and we have expected people to live by the standards and practices that we set within our particular religious tradition.

But the world has changed. How (and whether) we worship God, where we gather for religious ceremonies, how we express our faith has a wide diversity. The way to get our Christian message heard is not to denounce others. Not even Jesus did that. Even in the face of criticism of his message, he announced that he had come not to destroy the law but to fulfill it,[2] and that he had come to bring abundant life.

Consider whether and how the message of your congregation is a message that is life giving and life affirming for today. People might understand words of judgment from the church as bullying. What was once shared as a religious truth becomes viewed as an act of profanity and judgment. How much better it is in our congregations to share guidance and help to translate the gospel message into words and concepts that resonate within our culture today. A new day has dawned. We need not change the life-affirming message of Jesus, but we do well to find new language to share

2 Matthew 5:17.

it to create a new vitality. Our goal as congregations can be to speak with as much care, sensitivity, and clarity as Jesus did.

Using profanity (understood broadly as any language that demeans and belittles another) is not listed among the spiritual gifts, and in fact stems from the baser tendencies of our being that we are inviting Jesus to transform through the Holy Spirit. We can make it our goal to use words to reconcile rather than to alienate.

Five Dirty Words

In the church we often use five common words that have the result of alienating, manipulating, and pressuring others rather than uplifting them and bringing about reconciliation. These five words of exclusion and judgment are: should, ought to, must, have to, and need.

Each of these words communicates a negative spirit, a false message, or an obligatory intent. Each may be used to hype urgency or arm-twist, particularly in the context of stewardship. (Think of admonitions like, "You ought/must/should/need to give more!") Sometimes these words are thinly disguised threats that attempt to create unholy fear or guilt.

Words, therefore, can make a difference. How they are to be understood depends on how they are used. Whatever their purpose and intent, it is clear that some of our speech in the church comes across as lacking any invitational grace. And it is above all grace that we are privileged to communicate as Christians.

Language That Reflects the Spirit of Christ

Our challenge is to use language that reflects the Spirit of Christ. Ask yourself: Is the welcoming spirit of Christ embedded in my words? In the words of our congregation? Do I seek out the stranger, rather than the familiar faces? Do we do so as a church? Do we even notice the person standing off in the corner? Do we invite others to be part of the family of God (or the fellowship of Christ) by uttering words that lead to a defensive response or words that are redemptive, invitational, and life giving?

Think about how you and your congregation name others. Do you speak about "visitors"? Why do we call people who come to worship with us "visitors?" The word is an insider-outsider word, one that gives power firmly to the insider and treats the outsider as less than.

Bill recently attended worship in a United Church. People for the most part were quietly welcoming (a nod here and a smile there) but one welcome was most memorable. With great gusto and energy a person came from three rows back to blurt out loudly, with hand outstretched, during the "welcoming" action of passing the peace: "I saw there was a stranger in our midst." The intent may have been to welcome and acknowledge Bill's presence, but being called a stranger when one has been a part of the denomination for almost sixty years is hardly reassuring. "Visitors" and "strangers" are not strangers to God but deserve a joyous welcome. How much better it would be to substitute the word "guest," a term that implies that the person is welcome figuratively and literally to sit and eat with us.

"Guests" receive preferential treatment, the kind of treatment God reserved for unique and special opportunities. A guest at our dinner table is served first and with particular honor and attention. We would never say to a guest we love and welcome fully: "You may be a vegetarian, but in our household you will eat meat or eat nothing." A guest is one we welcome into our midst.

As you become more conscious of the language you use in church, other words that are now outdated or even have negative connotations will no doubt come to mind. For example, "youth" is more positive than "teenager" these days, and "hymn" sounds more archaic than "worship music." Many denominations have for such reasons updated their song books. Martin Luther himself used popular song-tunes of his day, and gave them new meaning by attaching to them scriptural words and themes. Does our music inspire? Do our words ring true? Even Christian rappers are making a mark in the religious community through their words and themes. Take a look and listen to the YouTube rap entitled: Deepening Community Rap. The video was sponsored by Tamarack, a group that does community development work. The music was written and performed by Nathan Martin, whose mother is a minister of music. Nathan himself is schooled in all types of music, including religious, classical, jazz, and now rap. It is but one example of a new generation finding new ways to express the message of hope. We ignore such innovations at our peril.

"Church": A Highly Misunderstood Word

Our experience is that the word "church" is one of the most misunderstood words when used by members and leaders of faith communities. It is misunderstood because there are more than twenty different meanings of the word, and we seldom clarify which of those meanings we are using.

The word "church" can have any of the following meanings:[3]

1. A building that is set aside for religious purposes rather than residence or business, e.g., "the church food pantry/charity," or "the church as a place where people worship"
2. A theology of spiritual community, e.g., "The nature of the church, or marks of the church"
3. An address to know where to meet someone, e.g., "I'll take you to, or pick you up at, the church"
4. A community asset, e.g., "First Baptist Church is a place for many events and activities in the neighborhood"
5. A safe place, or place of spiritual renewal, e.g., "going to church for confession," "go to the nearest church"
6. A place of protection, as when an individual or family grouping is seeking refuge: "The family from the Sudan has found sanctuary in the local church"
7. A place where the organization's secretary works, e.g., "turn the paperwork in to the church office"
8. A congregation, e.g., "St. John's Lutheran Church"
9. The body of Christ, e.g., "Jesus Christ is the head of the church"
10. A denomination, e.g., "The United Methodist Church"
11. A grouping of denominations in contrast to other world religions, e.g., "the broader church" An inclusive broader religious entity, e.g., "the Protestant church"
12. A global theological or cultural religious group, e.g., "the Christian Church"

3 These definitions are compiled from many sources and are not intended to seem original.

13. A historically defined term, e.g., "the medieval church and/or the post-Reformation Church"
14. A hierarchical organization, e.g., "I work for the church"
15. A time of worship, e.g., "I'll see you at nine o'clock church"
16. A source of public ministry or advocacy, e.g., "the social statements of the church"
17. A moral standard or preferred kind of behavior, e.g., "church discipline"
18. A synonym for a mid-level judicatory, e.g., "a Synod, district, Presbytery, diocese of the church"
19. A source of truth, e.g., "What does the church say about that?"
20. A scapegoat for anything that is wrong, e.g., "The whole problem with the church is..."
21. A place to learn and develop values, e.g., "Where did we fail? We sent our kids to church"
22. A unique construct for an entity that is organizationally human and theologically divine
23. A value-laden term that denotes sacred rather than secular, or a place that demands a preferred kind of behavior, e.g., "Don't do that in church!" Or, "How can you talk that way in church?"

Confusion and conflict increase with the number of meanings a word has. So, unless we specifically differentiate how we are using the term, we suggest changing how we use the word "church" to mean only two of the above: "congregation" and "the body of Christ." The New Testament uses the term "church" primarily with these two meanings. What is significant about these meanings is that they both refer to real people, living beings, a community of believers, and unique beings created by God. The emphasis is on *people* who work together in faith for a common good, and not on a group primarily with opposition to others. Even without a building, even if a particular congregation disbands, the church as the people of God exists. We simply connect with another faith community that is part of the worldwide body of Christ. And that congregation, we believe, will never close its doors.

The Worldwide Impact of Congregations

When we ask a group of people to name the organization that has had, and continues to have, the greatest impact on the world throughout history, some people say it's the Roman Empire. Others say it's Apple, or Microsoft. Still others mention General Motors, or Exxon. All of these organizations have certainly had a great impact on the world.

We submit, however, that the organization that has had the greatest impact in the history of the world, at least the last two thousand years, is the congregation. Congregations in every hamlet, town, or city have provided the glue that has held those communities together throughout the centuries. Congregations have banded together to form educational institutions, hospitals, social agencies, and have provided relief for global causes such as disasters and world hunger.

Congregations did all that. At various times in their history, they exemplified working together for the good of all, and they did it at less cost than others. Congregations can be change agents in their communities, so we should not refer to the future of congregations in desperate terms. Talk about how congregations are merely "hanging on" is not inspirational.

We believe that the congregation continues to have the greatest potential of all organizations for impacting the world today. Admittedly we have not always worked together as well as we could have. In times of persecution, moral decay, greed, and runaway consumerism, some congregations have given in to temptation and have retreated into self-preservation rather than continue to make it their primary goal to do God's mission.

This principle is foundational for our understanding of both *why* congregations need to be revitalized and *how* congregations can be revitalized. And neither the purpose nor the process of revitalization can be encapsulated in a program. Congregation renewal and revitalization is an ongoing, lifelong, God-given purpose for which the "church" was brought into being.

Now some may argue that we should not be isolated in our thinking. What about our denominational identity? What about sharing our faith beyond our local community borders? To such people we respond that the whole purpose of a denomination is to support and encourage congregations in sharing God's mission, and in spreading the gospel. Typically when we focus on preserving structures, or governance systems, or denominational order, the gospel is diminished, and we all suffer.

We invite you to help revitalize congregations in order to reconcile the world to God in Jesus Christ.[4] This principle also previews how the body of Christ will be revitalized. Revitalization of congregations is the Holy Spirit's way of being a Christian congregation. Congregation renewal is ongoing revitalization through the Holy Spirit. It is lifelong. It is the purpose of our life journey. Sometimes revitalization calls for sacrifice.

Ed's father was a missionary in Brazil. He often sacrificed to bring people into relationship with God. When he was asked, "What was the most important thing that you did?" he readily replied, "It was proclaiming the good news of Jesus Christ for the reconciling of the world to God. But I would rather have you ask, "What did you do that made the greatest impact on the world?" And the answer to that question would be, "After I was rejected by the people as being a witch doctor for suggesting it, I showed them how to dig wells to provide clean water that reduced infant mortality and increased health outcomes, and simply set that example as a follower of Jesus Christ."

Conclusion: The Primacy of the Congregation

Human organizations like churches will always be flawed, imperfect, at times undependable, and not always laudable. On the other hand, the congregation, the imperfect yet forgiven people, the dependable yet undependable, the capable in spite of all their incapacities, is still the greatest hope for the fulfillment of God's mission. "God was in Christ reconciling the world unto himself through Jesus Christ and has committed unto us that ministry of reconciliation."[5]

Paradoxical as it is, the congregation is where the reality of God's mission on this earth comes into being. Once we decide to communicate in a redemptive and life-giving way, we remind ourselves and others that the congregation is a vibrant, wholesome, God-believing and justice-seeking community of believers.

4 2 Corinthians 5:19–21.
5 2 Corinthians 5:19–20.

Equally important, we equip each other to sort things out in a relationship community. We develop mutual accountability for how we talk and how we act. When we are mutually accountable we strengthen and protect each other from excess, and we encourage each other to boldness in God's grace. We grow when, rather than creating God in our image, we return to the basic tenet that we are created in God's image, as are also our neighbors.[6] By cleaning up our language and speaking the truth about humans as beloved by God, it becomes easy to inspire, uplift, and energize people to live their faith here and now.

If this is a wake-up call for you and could be a wake-up call for your congregation, embrace it, at least for the time being, as you discover how this all fits together and how it might be God-pleasing.

FOR FURTHER DISCUSSION

1. When was the last time you heard someone use profanity, whether it was blaming, name-calling, belittling, or cursing? How did you feel? Did you just let it go?

2. How does profanity hinder effective communication? How might you set the table for effective communication to occur?

3. Review the various meanings of "church." How might the word "congregation" (local) or the phrase "body of Christ" (broader) better describe your mission-shaped group?

4. What guidelines for effective conversation would you suggest to help your congregation carry out God's mission of reconciliation?

5. Congregations are living, breathing organisms that seek to share life with others. How is your congregation life-giving? Habitually using what new words might change its culture to become more life giving?

6 J. B. Phillips, *Your God Is Too Small.*

2

Hanging On and Letting Go

"Someone in the crowd said to him, 'Teacher, tell my brother to divide the family inheritance with me.' "But he said to him, 'Friend, who set me to be a judge or arbitrator over you?' And he said to them, "Take care! Be on your guard against all kinds of greed."[1]

The Illusion of Need

"I need a new car."

"I need a bigger house."

"I need more money."

"I need to be needed."

These statements are obviously not statements about real need. They are simply wants dressed up as if they were needs. On a deeper level, just using the word "need" disguises a basic characteristic of an unhealthy personality. A felt need is simply a subjective need to need.

A primary starting point in conflict management is to ask the question "Is the presenting issue the real issue?" In other words, is there a different, more foundational underlying cause to the problem? For example, a popular reason that is listed for divorce is "irreconcilable differences." The erroneous assumption is that differences have to be reconciled. It is better to assume that effective marriages handle their differences, or live with them. The fact is we do not always agree on everything. And that is fine. The way God designed life was not by making it mandatory to agree

1 Luke 12:13-15a.

with one another, but by making us capable of understanding each other, listening to different viewpoints, and learning from them.

Eliminating the Need to Need

Long ago we should have dispelled the notion that someone else can make us feel a certain way. Yes, people may lure us into difficult and even dangerous situations, yet we still control how we will react to such situations. People may try to make us angry, or make us feel incompetent, or unloved, or unimportant, but we do not have to give in to such bullies. A good sense of self enables us to react in positive, life-affirming ways and stand up for ourselves.

A congregation is no different. Each one of the congregations we have served has had its own unique personality. Sometimes the personality is shaped by those who have offered leadership (ministerial or lay); sometimes those personalities have been shaped by experiences they have shared (a major fire, the loss of a beloved member or members in some kind of disaster, a meaningful mission project); and sometimes the personalities of these congregations have grown in ways no one understands or has evaluated. They simply have become who they are. Just as it is important for each one of us to understand who we are and how we have become that way in life, so it is important for congregations to understand who they are and what makes them tick.

An axiomatic principle of systems theory (or how any kind of system works, from a family to a corporation) is self-differentiation as a healthy way of handling one's feelings. Just as the need to need is an illusion, so also is the need to be isolated or the need to be enmeshed. Anyone can be self-differentiated. What we mean by that is that we do not need to go into either of two ditches: 1) the irresponsible ditch that attempts to avoid reality, through escapism and separation; or 2) the bondage ditch of allowing ourselves to be dominated by another, surrendering our individuality. Neither do we need to harbor the illusion that we can handle tension and disagreement by seeking to control others, and forcing people to act as we expect. In this last scenario, we do not handle differences effectively; instead we dismiss or ignore the differences or overpower the people with whom we are in disagreement.

Like individuals, congregations can also be clear about who they are and how they function. It is important for them to be clear about what they hold as most meaningful. If the gospel is not at the top of what is important to our congregations, then we have some significant work to do together.

Our experience is that congregations tend to careen from one style of ministry to another because they seek the opposite of what they had before. So, if they have had a series of short-term, less than effective ministries, then they typically seek someone who will lead them in a stable way and for a long time. Yet effective ministry is not really a matter of style, but a matter of having a clear purpose and mission. When a congregation is clear about what the nature and goal of that particular community of faith is, and how leadership can support and enhance that ministry, then it is likely to be effective.

We suggest that the transformational principle—"letting go and holding on"—is vital and urgent to correct some of the weaknesses of organized religion. The gospel message itself is about letting go and holding on. We have an opportunity to let go of worries, fears, disappointment, and uncertainties in order to hold onto a faith that accepts God with confidence and with humility. Picture a canoe, with two guides, one in back with primary control to set direction, and one in front to help paddle. If we try to be in control, we will fail. God needs to be in control. Of course, if we stop taking a role in our faith journey, we will fail, for God's control is not about forcing us into actions we are not prepared to take, but more like the paddle or rudder at the back of the canoe helping to steer the vessel down the river. We all need to be paddling to share the journey.

In What Direction are You Paddling?

This principle of sharing in the paddling reminds Bill of an early paddling experience during his ordination charge in northeastern Ontario. The community of Manitouwadge (which means "cave of the Great Spirit") was then a mining town situated on a lovely lake by the same name: Lake Manitouwadge. On a sunny, calm afternoon he and his wife Ann headed out to canoe on the small lake. Suddenly the winds whipped up and the clouds rolled in. Clearly it was important to get to shore; the nature of small lakes means that they can become very rough very quickly once a storm comes.

Ann and Bill struggled as they headed the borrowed canoe into the waves and passed by a point that heralded a small cove where trees would protect them from the wind. As they reached the point, Bill remarked, "Well done, we will make it now," at which point Ann lifted up her paddle and sighed, "Thank goodness." Of course, what Bill had meant was that at that point he was sure they would make it *if they kept paddling*. Without Ann paddling, the canoe was quickly swept into the middle part of the lake, and the return to shore became even more challenging.

So it is in our congregations. We all need to continue paddling in the same general direction or we will get swept off course by the storms that inevitably arise around us.

The decline of mainline denominations has many causes. We suggest that one underlying current of unhealthy thinking that contributes greatly to this decline is our unwillingness or inability to handle our feelings, thoughts, and actions in a healthy way. It is troubling when someone in a mall parking lot becomes enraged over a driver who is parking too slowly for the other person's desire, but it is even more upsetting to see such vitriol expressed in a congregation meeting or a worship planning session.

Many congregations set themselves up to be victimized in these ways by imitating dysfunctional family systems. How can we recognize when our congregational system is not working, and what can we do to change our dysfunctional congregational behaviors? To answer this, let us first explore what it means to be dysfunctional or "at risk."

What Does it Mean That a Congregation is 'At Risk?'

In organized religion we have come to classify congregations as being "at risk" simply because they have fallen below some arbitrary minimum average of weekly worshipers. Size does not determine risk. A small congregation is no more at risk than a larger congregation. True, a minimum number of people is necessary for basic sustainability. But it is equally accurate to say that many small congregations are truly helpful congregations and they have every reason to be as sustainable as any larger congregation.

Size-theory is not determinative. What is essential is understanding who we are as a people of God, and living the gospel in the context of that community of faith.

A congregation in Western Kansas had an average attendance of thirteen per week. One member covered a majority of the funding that the congregation needed. It was not solely the fact that the donor was eighty-four years old that made the congregation unsustainable, but also the fact that the members were resigned to the idea that when this donor died the congregation would close its doors. They were so enmeshed in this assumption that their only concern was how, when the church closed, to provide for the perpetual care of the cemetery behind the building. This thought process was the reason for closing the doors. It is understandable that such unsustainable thinking will close the doors of an organization. Things turned around when this congregation joined in conversation with five other congregations to consider how they might serve God better together than by themselves. In 2014 these six congregations celebrated their tenth anniversary of still being viable by working together in mission.

What it Takes to Become a Sustainable Congregation

Determination and Commitment: The Example of the First Maundy Thursday

On the night before Jesus was crucified, the eleven disciples were gathered in the upper room. They observed the Lord's Supper, also called the Last Supper. They washed each other's feet, and if they had had a business meeting they likely would have decided that they needed to close their doors and disband. Such a final congregation meeting would also have been understandable because they had pretty good reason to believe that their leader would be executed within twenty-four hours.

So how was it that this small band of followers of Jesus would become the body of Christ that today encompasses millions of disciples throughout the world?

Business and industry rightly make such decisions on the basis of statistics, profit, and loss. But do you tell a toddler who is trying to walk, "Give up. You will not walk today"? The determination and commitment to take that first step will usually override any external discouragement. "Unless we become like little children, we shall not enter the Kingdom of God."

Finding Our Passion and Keeping Our Doors Open

We are not suggesting that any congregation that closes its doors should be judged for doing so. The only point of these examples is that they foreground the presenting issue rather than the underlying problem. To put it another way, if you're going to be bothered by just about anything, it is likely that you can also give up on just about anything for just about any reason. The flipside is also true. When someone says that we want to "keep churches from closing their doors" that can be an equally flawed example of a presenting issue. The issue is not "Are the doors open or shut?" or "Does this church have the funds to stay open?" but "Is the congregation living its purpose through sharing God's hope with the world?"

We suggest that many congregations who have closed their doors over presenting issues could have kept their doors open and become thriving congregations by using principles of transformational leadership.

What is essential for the future of the congregation is not numbers, not financial security, not just an improved understanding of the gospel, nor even a new housing development in one's neighborhood. All of these may be helpful in providing the resources and the people toward reaching the overall goal of living a vibrant faith within the congregational community. But what is crucial is whether we have the passion to live as followers of Jesus Christ. To have the passion means we are ready to share in God's mission. As in any organization, the biggest asset we have as a congregation is not the size of the community or the abundance of the treasury; it is the passion to carry out our call and purpose—as Christians. Today, however, even that passion is not enough. We must be willing to be transformed for a new time and a new reality.

Passion breeds success

In an interview Bobby Orr talked about his success as a hockey player.[2] Arguably the greatest defenseman in the history of that game, Orr has

2 Maclean's Magazine, October 28, 2013.

written a new book on hockey that has some critical things to say about the way young hockey players are developed today. When asked, "What is the reason for your success?" Orr is very clear: "The love and passion that I had for the game was it for me." He goes on to suggest that today parents and coaches often suck the passion out of children by being unrealistic in their expectations, or by humiliating the child with their critical comments.

In congregations, that translates to a passion about the gospel. When we spend our time ranting on about what people do not give, or do not offer, or do not share, then we simply humiliate those new to the congregation and do not provide them with opportunities to grow as we hope.

If our very first statement to a new person who comes through our doors were a simple: "Welcome, thank you for being here today" and that statement were followed up with a genuine welcoming attitude, many more would return to our congregations. The challenge for those who are new to our places of worship is that what they see and experience is a long way from what they seek: good news.

Passion generates energy

When I am passionate about doing something, whether it is taking a stand or lending a hand, I do not lack energy. Underlying every presenting issue, positive or negative, there is a driving energy-producing force called passion. Creative ideas flow form a passion that creates resurrection energy that can turn defeat into victory. The Holy Spirit specializes in all those areas.

When a couple of people are in conversation in the name of Jesus Christ, God's Spirit is in the conversation with them. God gives us the creativity and passion to develop ideas as well as the resurrection energy to carry them out in God's name.

The congregation in Western Kansas with a weekly average worship attendance of thirteen through just such conversation discovered their new future as an important part of a six-congregation parish. Four of the other five congregations were in the same boat, all at risk of closing their doors.

Today that combined parish is alive and well. They have more qualified staff members together than they had when they were apart. They have a vision for God's mission, a passion that had not surfaced earlier. Because they thought transformationally, their attitude changed from despair to hope. Each congregation discerns the unique gifts that they brought to the parish. That became the criterion for what it means to be "sustainable."

Of course it is possible that someday the entire parish will close its doors. But if it does, it will do so in a way that expands God's mission. They now know how to think transformationally.

Thinking Transformationally Rather than Sequentially

The first step in this transformational leadership principle is to "*Let Go of Everything that Bothers You.*" As the Bible puts it bluntly, "Don't be bothered by anything, not even the wicked."[3]

Letting go of everything that bothers you is an umbrella principle. Internalize this principle and you will find that several other transformational leadership principles that we discuss in this chapter/book fall in line underneath it. The trust principle comes to life. The paradox of taking your time yet acting quickly becomes clear. On the other hand, when you ignore this principle, other areas of your life fall apart too.

Whatever bothers us, or upsets us, or creates abnormal anxiety in us, holds us hostage. Being bothered puts our brains in handcuffs and distracts us from our purpose and mission. When we are upset, distracted, or anxious, we hinder ourselves. We slow down and we need more time than usual to accomplish our simplest tasks and our broader purpose. And we make any task more difficult. Anxiety keeps us from thinking clearly and keeps us from focusing on specifics. Why not let go of everything that bothers us? Why do we allow ourselves to be bothered by anything?

The story of Jesus healing the woman burdened and stooped over in Luke's gospel is a symbol of how we in the congregation handle our lives. Jesus says the woman's condition is the result of the action of Satan, and urges those around her not to dismiss the burden she has carried. Too often, however, we have opened ourselves to burdens that bring us to our knees when we have failed to be open to the presence of God in our midst.

We can get caught up in procedural fixes for the latest presenting challenge. This is as dangerous in the congregation as in businesses or

3 Psalm 37:1.

education or in a neighborhood. Too easily we forget that we have the presence of God to support us and to help us face whatever burden comes our way. Jesus continually taught those who came to him that God is with us; we are not alone. We do not need to carry our burdens and concerns alone. So why do we often seek the "fixes" within our communities and congregations alone?

How did this biblical woman become overwhelmed by her burdens? How have we become stooped and discouraged? There are at least a couple of reasons why we are bothered and discouraged. The first reason is that we are simply immaturely choosing to be bothered. Now, if someone intentionally wants to be bothered by something, we say, "That's fine; you have the power to make that choice." When I was young I allowed myself to be bothered by many things without realizing the consequences I was bringing on myself. I blamed others. I made excuses for myself. It was as though I made a list called, "Reasons for Not Looking Good." How silly is that?

I no longer choose to do that. Fortunately, I learned a way that is more helpful for me. Sometimes I still get bothered by trivial things I call "paper clip size" issues. As the book title asks, "Who Moved My Cheese?" When I become aware that I'm bothered I can ask myself, "What bat boy put that program together?"

Choosing Not to Get Upset

The second reason for being bothered is more sinister. Ed tells the story of how, early in his marriage, he often got upset with his wife. Here is Ed's story, in his own words:

> *One night, over lemonade with my friend Lowell, I shared how upset I was with my wife. Lowell let me vent a while. I listed examples that were intended to justify my reasons for getting upset with my wife. Then he asked, "Ed, why do you get upset with your wife?" I thought that was a silly question, since I had just given him a bunch of reasons, so I responded, "I just gave you many reasons. If you were married to her, you would feel the same way!'"*
>
> *Lowell cut to the chase. "Yes, I might, but that is not the point. I don't think you heard what I asked you. Is the reason you get upset with*

her because you get a payoff? When you get upset with your wife, could it be because then you get your way?'

I will never forget that moment. The question jolted me in the deepest part of my heart. It was obvious that I was manipulating her by getting upset in order to get my way. In that moment I was brought to my knees. I never wanted to be that kind of husband again. I wanted to be free of whatever it was in me that manipulated others to get my way.

Often what really upsets us about others' behavior is that it reminds us of our own behavior. Often the people most like us are the people we find a challenge to work with, because they may appear to do things as we do, but for some reason another person can never be as complete or as perfect as we see ourselves being. But once we realize that we judge most harshly those most like us, then we realize that patience with others is a foretaste of what it might be like if we were more accepting and forgiving of ourselves.

Then again, sometimes we are irked by those who are doing the very thing we would like to do but somehow cannot. I have a good friend who spends many an evening quietly at home with her partner. She speaks with fondness of how much she enjoys the quiet times they spend together. There have been times when I thought they should do more, go more places, be active in more community events, but then one day I realized my expectations for them were borne of my own desire to have a life closer to the one they live. I would like more evenings at home, and more days off to do tasks around the house or pursue personal opportunities. I have structured my life so that those opportunities are rare, and at times I resent that. But whose fault is it? It is my own doing. So why should I complain about other people who have been careful to organize their personal lives in such a way that they can enjoy what is important to them? There is no reason for me to be angry or frustrated by others who have made their own clear-thinking choices. The simple truth is: I can stay at home more, too, if that is what I really want.

We see this "anger-sickness" not only in individuals' lives but also in communities and congregations. Councils are usually composed of competent leaders, and yet they are sometimes bothered over trivial issues, or angry at people who differ from them. Why do you think one council member can get his way simply by getting upset? At that moment, what happens to the council's capacity to deal with priorities in mission?

Choosing Not to Keep the Peace at all Costs

Congregation leaders often think their role is to keep the peace at all costs. It is not. Our purpose is to share the gospel at all costs. Just as Jesus at times caused confusion and dissention among his disciples as he shared a transformative message with them, so at times we will find the gospel message jarring and upsetting. Avoiding such experiences never allows a congregation to grow in its faith. We must face difficult issues with love and understanding, but we cannot avoid them. A community or a congregation board that puts peace and happiness above seeking to follow the ways of Jesus Christ and to preach the gospel with justice, clarity, and obedience will not be a successful community for long.

Early in his ministry Bill was asked how he keeps everyone happy and satisfied in his congregation. What was his secret? He replied that such a goal is impossible. "Perfection" in any leadership role within the congregation, he replied, is keeping 80% of the people happy 80% of the time.

Now he had no statistical basis for that comment, other than a strong hunch from his then limited experience. But after over twenty years of experience consulting with congregations in a variety of contexts, he has made that insight part of his package of truths worth sharing with leaders that seek congregational transformation.

Why those percentages? Well, if you do not keep close to 80% of the people happy and engaged 80% of the time, they may feel the ministry has failed to meet their ongoing needs. They may not experience the congregation as a place that includes them. And if a leader or minister seeks to keep more than 80% of the people happy, or seeks almost unanimous comfort, then the preaching and prophetic ministry of the congregation clearly is lacking. We may be comforting the afflicted, but we have lost the gospel edge to afflict the comfortable. Being comfortable is not a congregational goal in a healthy congregation; being faithful is.

To that extent, many of our congregations have not failed in becoming more modern in their approach but rather have forgotten the reason for their being. We exist to share the gospel of Jesus Christ. The methodology by which the gospel is shared may need to change; but the power of the gospel message remains constant.

Breaking the Cycle of Winning and Losing

Yes, the gospel message at times can set us on edge and make us feel uncomfortable. We need to face that reality.

What often happens in the congregation, however, is that we let superficial concerns and issues bother us, and so we avoid the important concerns that arise out of the gospel in our deliberations and in our gatherings. When we allow something to bother us we set ourselves up to become victims. And the more we allow ourselves to be bothered, the more frequently it will happen and with more serious results. Resisting it doesn't help. What we resist intensifies the energy; what we embrace diminishes it.

It is not transformational to get upset. The amazing transformational principle is "let go of everything that bothers you." Let go of it. When we are controlled by our negative emotions, we are held captive by the person who aroused such a response. That person or group who has set us on edge, derailed our course of action, has gleefully looked on as we lost our sense of purpose.

Letting go of whatever bothers us breaks the cycle of "winning" and "losing." We should stop worrying about the "how" or process of ministry and remind ourselves of the "what" of ministry. We are to be a justice seeking people. When that becomes our focus, a lot of the details of congregational life become less problematic. Let go of the petty worries and arguments; retain the essence of the gospel of Jesus Christ, and hold on to its message. That is why we say "let go and hold on."

Choosing to Downsize

When Bill planned a move from northern Ontario to Toronto, a relocation which involved moving from a large house with four bedrooms and a study into a flat with one small bedroom, he was forced to downsize significantly.

He sold about two thirds of his furniture and possessions. Because he wanted to keep his library, it meant he could no longer maintain most of his furniture and art work.

He had a choice: he could send the art to auction, or he could give away various pieces to colleagues, friends, and people who shared his passion for art. In the end, people who loved art and enjoyed some of the paintings and prints that he once had hanging from the walls of his house received unexpected art gifts that last Christmas in the community.

Bill learned a principle that many Jesus-followers have learned. What a joy it was to give those art pieces away! Some originally were pricey (at least in the eyes of a minister, though none would have made Sotheby's auction list), and even the more modestly priced pieces were treasured favorites. Bill was giving away these treasures. Yet the loving way in which others received these treasures was a joy beyond belief. Sounds like the buried treasure in Jesus' parable, doesn't it?

Many of us have congregations that sit in large buildings on prominent corners in the towns and cities of North America, or hold extensive land resources worth millions of dollars in suburban areas, or have the only community building in a rural region facing depopulation. These buildings remain tombs for buried treasures, because we are afraid of (or incapable of) sharing the gospel openly and freely. After all, the gospel is the true asset of our faith.

Bill now is going through a similar process once again–returning to that same one-bedroom flat after working in another community where he rented a fairly large two-bedroom apartment. Again, he has given away furniture to agencies that help those in transition, mothers and children leaving abusive relationships, or recent refugees relocating to his country. Again he will cull his art collection, for he is at a stage in life where storing beautiful paintings in a box long term serves no one. He is adamant that none of it will be sold, but what is surplus will be given away, because that is the only way that he can both honor the art and celebrate the value of it. It is so valuable to him that he must give it away; selling it will only cheapen it.

How did that principle of giving things away become so clear to him? Years ago in his first exercise of downsizing, he did send some pieces to auction as well as give away others. One piece, in particular, was a much-loved Group of Seven numbered print, done by Tom Thomson. In Canada, the artwork of the so-called Group of Seven symbolizes the Canadian heritage. Originals sell for tens of thousands of dollars, so even numbered prints can be fairly costly.

He had been pleased to get this particular piece for less than $300 at auction. When it sold for $50, the auctioneer congratulated him on this old picture selling for such a fine price. Bill was devastated. The auctioneer could not understand Bill's response when he blurted out: "I should have given it away." But at $50, minus 30% auctioneer fees, Bill would receive only $35 for the picture. What joy that picture could have given a friend and art connoisseur if Bill had only realized that letting go was the best way to hold on to the special nature of this art. Bill is determined not to make the same mistake again.

Identifying What Really Matters to Us

Now all of that emotion may seem too intense for the simple story shared, but congregations often make a big deal about relatively small possessions, don't they? As Bill did with the Tom Thomson print, we put far more value on items than we do on serving and sharing with people. We need to change.

Those who want to share will give generously and joyfully. Giving joyfully can be liberating for the receiver and for the giver. "Lighten up!" is the best stewardship principle there can be. Challenges in the congregation, like aged Abraham and Sarah receiving word that they will soon have a child, often deserve a good laugh.

Well, that is good advice, but I don't find it so easy myself. When I am giving a presentation to a group, and my wife is present, she will regularly communicate to me with some kind of semaphoric gesture that shouts, "You're too serious. Smile." That's code for, "Let go of your need to control and change others."

Real personal growth can happen when we give things away (such as art or books or ideas) simply because we want to share joy with someone else. Real growth in the congregation happens when we share who we are and what we have with anyone in need, when we share the gospel without expecting something in return.

Dr. Phil regularly asks people who get upset, "How's that working for you?" His simple intent is to get people to ask, "What's the big deal? Why do I get upset?"

Richard Carlson wrote a book, *Don't Sweat the Small Stuff: It's All Small Stuff.* His intent is to help us conquer our little habits, like getting upset, or worrying, habits that sap us of our energy and joy.

When we can get to the point that we see our implementation of programs and activities as the small stuff, and the faith that empowers us and provides purpose in our lives as the significant truth, then we can begin to think and act in transformational ways. Yet often we lock our faith into our actions and programs, rather than letting them be distinct and separate. Programs and activities build community, camaraderie, and cooperation. Faith builds hope, vision, passion, commitment, and renewed life.

Letting Go Does Not Make Our Beliefs Less Appealing to Others

We understand that there are important matters of theology that warrant our taking a stand. But just because we feel strongly about something does not justify our becoming bothered about it. Our current beliefs can, after all, change. Bill Easum says, "Sacred Cows Make Gourmet Burgers." Chill out. Ps 46:10 says, "Be still and know that I am God." Matthew 6:34 says, in Eugene Peterson's words, "Don't get worked up about what may or may not happen." You have heard of arteriosclerosis, the hardening of the arteries. Getting upset is the "hardening of the attitudes!" Letting go does not make our beliefs less appealing to others.

What a difference it would make if the motto of our congregations would change from "We seek to be *right* at all costs" to "We seek to be *light* at all costs."

Later on we will describe in greater depth how this applies to conflict management. Suffice it to say at this point that principle is transformational also in how it applies to both individual conflict management and systemic conflict management in congregations.

For many people, this principle is transformational for themselves and for their congregations. It is a wake-up call of the highest order. And it is God-pleasing.

FOR FURTHER DISCUSSION

1. When have you felt bullied in your life? How did you overcome it?
2. How does your congregation start new ministries and discontinue obsolete ones? What changes would you make in that decision-making style to help your congregation?
3. The story of the canoe reminds us that "paddling together" is not always the same as "paddling in the same way," for we each have our own role in moving the congregation forward. How might your congregation give the clear message that you are "paddling together" for the good of the gospel? How do you make room for welcoming new participants—paddlers or riders?
4. If the Gospel is a precious gift for us, how can we see our purpose as Christians as giving away something valuable?
5. What is your favorite memory of giving someone something that was valuable? How did you feel about making that gift?

3

Taking on More and Respecting Our Limits

"Thus the heavens and the earth were finished, and all their multitude. And on the 7th day God finished the work that he had done, and he rested on the 7th day from all the work that he had done."[1]

Trust God—But Don't Unplug Your Brain

You may know the story about the man who believed that God would rescue him from an impending flood. A police car drove by the houses and shouted to all residents over a loudspeaker, "There is a flood coming today. It will fill the whole valley with water! Evacuate as soon as possible!" The man heard the announcement, stayed on his porch, and told the police, "God will rescue me."

The water level rose and surrounded his house, and all the roads were closed. "You must evacuate immediately!" a nearby canoeist called out to him. "The flood will destroy your home and you will drown if you don't get into the canoe right now!" The man shouted from an upstairs window, "God will rescue me."

The flood was raging through the valley. A helicopter with a loudspeaker broadcast the warning, "Evacuate at once! This is your last chance. If you don't leave now, you will trapped in the flood." The man heard the warning as he was standing on his roof. He waved at the helicopter and shouted, "God will rescue me."

The man drowned. When he met God, he complained, "You promised that you would provide for my every need! Why didn't you rescue me?"

1 Genesis 2:1-2.

God replied, "I did provide for your every need. Three times! I sent you a police car, a canoe, and a helicopter."

We often hear that story repeated, and we always know how it's going to turn out. But we still smile every time we hear it. We understand that trusting in God is no excuse to unplug your brain.

Trusting God 100% is Transformational

Jesus said, "If you have faith as small as a mustard seed, you will say to this mountain, "Move from here to there, and it will move; and nothing shall be impossible for you."[1] This is the fulcrum around which everything else transformational revolves.

Do you stumble over this verse and say, "You can't trust in God 100%? What are you talking about?" Of course you can. Through the Holy Spirit, you are free to trust God 100%. Don't worry about anything. Don't be afraid of anything, and keep a healthy respect.

Let go of everything that bothers you. If you believe this principle, you are on your way to becoming a transformational leader. We utter truths we hold dear in our congregation, such truths as "God is our rock and salvation" and "God's spirit always surrounds us and guides us," but how much do we really believe such words? Our actions belie our beliefs.

We Do Not Need a Lot of Faith to Make a Difference

Jesus used a mustard seed to represent the kind of faith we need. If we have faith even the size of a mustard seed, we can accomplish great things.

Have you actually seen a mustard seed? Jesus used the symbol of a mustard seed because he was good at turning upside down the images of the traditional religion of his day. While some looked to priests and rulers for images of power and greatness, Jesus advocated that we become like little children to enter into the kingdom of heaven.[2] While the biblical witness uses images of the cedars of Lebanon and the mighty oak as representative of greatness, Jesus used the example of a mustard seed.

Years ago I went to a local seed company and bought a small envelope of mustard seeds. There were enough seeds for each of the children in the

---

2 Luke 18:17.

Sunday school to have one seed. Mustard seeds weigh almost nothing at all and they are very tiny. The whole package of seed I bought that day cost eight cents.

Jesus was saying in his usually understated way: I am not asking you to have faith greater than the prophets and the religious leaders of this world. I want you to have faith that is hardly measurable in human terms, but is clear to God. We do not need a lot of faith to make a difference.

We make a mistake when we characterize the expectations we have of people as somehow being beyond their capacity. We simply must be aware that God has given us faith sufficient to live the gospel in our time and place. If we only need faith as large as a mustard seed to transform the world—or at least our community—then why are we so reluctant to be agents of transformation? It takes very little faith to act, but it does take *some* faith.

Trust is a Choice

People mistakenly tend to consider trust[3] as something that is earned. That is incorrect. Trust is a choice. Trust is letting go of control; it is surrender.

The story is told of the man who fell off a cliff, and as he was falling he shouted, "Is anyone up there? Save me!" A voice came in the darkness: "Reach out your hand and grab the tree branch!" And he did. "Thank you for saving me!" Before long, the man realized he couldn't hold onto the tree branch much longer, and again he shouted, "Is anyone up there? Save me!" The voice in the darkness returned and said, "Let go of the branch." The man cried out, "Is anybody else up there?" The man finally gave up in despair and let go of the tree branch. There was solid ground

3 We understand faith as being composed of three dynamics—knowledge, assent, and confidence. We know the facts. We give our allegiance to the principles. We simply act on them, and live into them. All three are forms of believing. For example, if we were to take the subject of speed limits, we would all agree that it is not sufficient to know about the subject. If we are driving, it is necessary to know what the speed limit is where we are at the moment. It is certainly important for us to comply with speed limits for our protection and for the protection of others. But neither of those two dynamics is helpful unless we actually drive within the speed limit. Ignorance is no excuse. We surrender our individualism to the greater wisdom. And we trust that wisdom by living it. Faith is not the absence of doubt, uncertainty, or fear. It is trusting, even in uncertainty, doubt, and fear.

right beneath him. He didn't even fall down, and was soon rescued. All he had to do was trust.

Trusting God is not blind trust; it depends fully on the promises of God. The promises of God are sure. The flip side of trusting God 100% is actively doing something including the principle "Trust and verify."[4]

It is true that you have to "earn other people's trust;" but that is only half the truth. If you have a track record of dependability, it is likely that your reputation developed over a period of time. You might even say that there is a statistical probability that you are trustworthy. But statistics are not particularly comforting. Indeed, "46.8% of all statistics are made up on the spur of the moment."[5] In fact, there is an equal and opposite principle called "the law of averages," that would indicate the higher the statistical probability that you can be trusted, the greater the likelihood that you will violate that trust.

Trust, even in the face of a flawless track record, is still a choice. This is God's way of trusting us. We are untrustworthy and God chooses to trust us, in spite of us. Have you thought about the possibility that trust is synonymous with forgiveness?

My wife trusts me not because I have earned her trust by never letting her down. She believes in me and trusts me to never let her down, knowing in her heart of hearts that it is just a matter of time before I let her down again.

She trusts that when I let her down, I feel worse about it than she does. I don't like myself when I let someone down. I am unhappy with myself when I let God down. There is nothing I can do to make up for letting someone down. There is no way that I can earn that trust back again. I have "broken that trust."

---

4 To ignore the nature of human nature is naïve. All of us need boundaries and ways of being disciplined to stay within those boundaries. For example, we measure the seriousness and the frequency of violating our boundaries, not only to provide consequences for the past, but also to prevent the recurrence of those violations in the future. If we agree to work together, we trust each other to carry out our commitment and we measure it and enforce it.

5 An imaginary statement that pokes fun of and misuses statistics. Footnoting it doesn't document it.

Trust May be the Greatest Motivator of All

One very important question that arises is, "What is it that I need when I have broken trust?" I might need correction, or take corrective action. But, I also need a hand that reaches down and says, "I forgive you," and lifts me up and tells me, "And I trust you again because I choose to do so." And I trust my wife the same way. All of this flows naturally out of the most important question of all, "What is it that God does every time we break the trust?" God forgives us in Jesus Christ. And God trusts us, as though it never happened, and as though it will never happen again. God gives me the capacity to trust. That is our trust, trusting in the promises of God. "Not one word has failed of all his good promises, which he spoke through his servant Moses."[6]

When someone trusts us, it creates a tremendous inner force that will do almost anything to justify that trust. When a blind man trusts you to lead him across the street, the power of that trust on you is immeasurable. When I participated in an exercise called the "blind walk," with a partner, and each of us could choose whether we wanted to begin by leading or being led, I chose to be led. I was blindfolded and held my partner's hand behind his back as he led me through the crowded room of dyads walking about. After I completed my turn to be led, it was my turn to lead. I put my hand behind my back and my partner held onto my hand and was blindfolded. As I led him through the crowded room of moving people, I felt a great sense of responsibility to keep him from bumping into anyone, whereas when he was leading me all I needed was simple trust. I concluded that there may be no greater motivation than to be trusted. Can you imagine that for you?

Trust is Sweet Surrender

It was this whole-hearted trust that came into Ed's heart during a difficult time. And the trust in God came through a popular song:

> *Sweet, sweet surrender; Live, live without care; like the fish in the water, like the birds in the air.*
>
> *Lost and alone on some forgotten highway; traveled by many remembered by a few.*

---

6 1 Kings 8:56.

Looking for something that I can believe in; looking for something I can do with my life.

There's nothing behind me and nothing before me that might've been true yesterday.

Tomorrow is open, and right now it's enough just to be here today.

Sweet, sweet surrender; Live, live without care; like the fish in the water, like the birds in the air.[7]

Sometimes our prayers take on the form of "give me, give me, and give me." It can be an amazing thing to see how our trust in God can grow, simply by changing our prayers from asking for everything we want to praising and thanking God for everything we already have and trusting him with our lives.

"I will praise the Lord with my whole heart, in the assembly of the upright, and in the congregation."[8]

"Trust in the Lord with all your heart; and lean not on your own understanding."[9]

Seeing is Believing vs. Believing is Seeing

The balancing principles for trust are a paradox. On the one hand, "Seeing is believing." On the other hand, believing is seeing "in spite of what we see." Jesus mentions both sides of the trust coin[10] when he talks to his disciple Thomas. When we believe, we will see. Jesus said, "If you have faith as small as a mustard seed, you will say to this mountain, "Move from here to there, and it will move; and nothing shall be impossible for you."[2] This is the axle around which transformation revolves.

Some people will push back: "You can't trust in God 100%. It's impossible." Of course we can't. None of us possesses the willpower to trust God all the time. On the other hand, you can trust God 100%. It's simple. The Holy Spirit lives in us, and we are free to trust God 100%. We can be free from worry, 100%. We can be free of fear, 100%. We can let go

---

7 Song by John Denver.
8 Psalm 111:1.
9 Proverbs 3:5.
10 John 20:29.

of everything that bothers us, 100%. If you believe this principle, you are on your way to becoming a transformational leader.

Trusting God is not blind trust; it is about depending fully on the promises of God. The promises of God are sure.

Now we move on to the flip side of trusting God 100%, and that is doing something!

Trust is Surrender...*and* Doing Something

That trust in God is not only about surrender but also about doing something may be the easiest transformation leadership principle to accept. It is certainly one that is reassuring. However, at face value, this principle can easily be misunderstood. So it is important to discuss this principle, not in contrast to education, but as a supplement to education.

Do we learn by memorizing principles? Or do we learn by living into our learning?

Two Kinds of Knowing: Knowledge and Action

The answer is, "Yes." We learn by knowing and by doing. Jesus says, "If you do... You will know..."[11] Real education is both.

Both of them are true, but in different ways. We might even say there are several kinds of truth—analytic truth, emotive truth, and synthetic truth. Just as a blind person can exclaim, "Oh, I see!," so after a person hears a joke, it sometimes takes him a while to get the punch line and exclaim, "Oh, I get it!" Jesus says, "If you know the truth, the truth will set you free." This knowing is both absolute and practical. It may take both to let go of getting upset. Jesus said, "If you DO... you will KNOW." Transformational leadership holds that faith includes knowledge, assent, and confidence.

Faith must be accompanied by action. No sitting on the fence. "But what if I don't know which way to go?" Get off the fence. As Yogi Berra said, "When you come to a fork in the road, take it."

---

11 John 7:17.

"But," you say, "what if I make the wrong decision?" You'll find out soon enough! In other words, we learn from experience, but sometimes it isn't long before we have to make a mid-course correction.

Follow Your God-Given Passion

The transformational principle requires some explanation: "Do what you really want to do; it may be your God-given passion." We are shifting the focus, not to be free to do whatever we want to do, but to be free to follow our God-given passion. Let's look at the what, why, and how of doing that.

The What

We ask children, "What do you want to be when you grow up?" This is the "passion principle." More recently we have calculated and discussed what children and young people should do based on the education needed, or the salary to be expected at the end of the process. Yet without a passion to do what one wants to do, a career choice can be very frustrating. The meaning of the word "vocation" is "calling." We aspire to know what our calling in life is. It is not a word only reserved for religious vocations. Without to some extent being aware of and following our calling we will not find fulfillment or purpose on earth.

Notice that there are two pivotal questions. What does God want me to do? How am I supposed to do it? The "what" question is answered by your passion. The "how" question is answered by your spiritual gifts. It is a simple principle. For more information, you might read a book on the subject.[12]

What would you do in life even if you didn't get paid for it? That's passion. Articulating one's desire is not always easy, particularly when the more specifically we can do so the better. Saying, "I'm a people person," is too general. What kind of people? What gender? What ethnic group? What social class? What age? What education? What interactions do you seek? What other characteristics would you like?

The woman who said, "My passion is to help children five to nine years old, who have learning disabilities or behavioral disorders, who don't feel like they belong," gave a pretty clear description of her passion.

12 Ed Kruse, *Unwrap Your Gifts and Use Them*, available from www.HealthierChurch.org

The Why

There is one other important aspect to our God-given passion, namely that it also answers the "why" question. Think like a Hebrew. They didn't ask, "How did God create the world and human beings?" The Hebrews asked, "Why?" Why did God create humans? Why did God create you? What is your why? Our "why" is to glorify God and build up the body of Christ. Our why is to share the gospel with clarity and with passion. In what way are you called to do that?

But even though we've answered the "what" question and the "why" question, that leaves one question still to discuss and that is the "how" question.

The How

Just as your passion answers your "What should I do?" question, your spiritual gifts answer the "How shall I do it?" question.

Think back to the first place you ever remember living. If you looked out the front door, what did you see? If you looked out the back door, what did you see? What is your earliest recollection of a yard? If you didn't have a yard, think of someone you knew who had a yard. Whether it was a big yard or a small yard doesn't matter. Your father or mother (or another relative) could tell you stories of the many ways your yard was important. An urban yard could consist of flowers and landscaping in the front and concrete in the backyard, a place to shoot baskets, with no grass. Or your yard may have been grass that needed to be mowed.

Bill lived in a house where the backyard contained a large garden but the yard also was big enough to have neighborhood ball tournaments and winter hockey games on a natural ice surface. Everyone felt welcomed in this backyard.

Do people feel welcomed in your place of worship, or in the space where you gather as a community during the week?

We hope your yard or neighborhood was a place of safety. As long as you were in your yard, you were home. Likely, if you were born before 1960, you knew where your parents were. Your parents knew where you were. They knew where they could find you. It was a place of freedom. You could do almost anything you wanted in your own yard. You could build things, make things, play with different things, climb things, or just sit and look at things.

Consider your "yard" as a metaphor for one of your earliest boundaries. Think of your yard as a metaphor for your spiritual boundary in serving God. In your own yard, and the yards of neighboring children, you could develop skills, learn about your gifts and limitations, and explore new opportunities. You figured out what you were good at, and what you should set aside. (Bill's boxing career ended with him getting a bloody nose in a neighbor's backyard trying out their new set of boxing gloves.)

Your spiritual gifts answer the "how" question. This frees you, enables you, and empowers you to say "no" when you are asked to do something, just because it does not fit with your gifts. It is also helpful to be aware of what your gifts are, so that you can effectively and joyfully use those gifts that are God-given in ways that support and encourage others. Know your spiritual gifts. Take a spiritual gifts inventory.[13]

I hope the twin principles of "passions" and "gifts" have stimulated you to learn more about them. If you identify your passions and gifts, you have a head start on becoming a transformational leader.

From Individual to Congregation Gifts

Of course, it is not only an individual but a congregation that has spiritual gifts. These identify them as a community, or as a family. It is a tremendous advantage for your congregation members to know their passions and gifts. If you equip your congregation to identify and know their spiritual gifts and passions, this will help them to become a transformational congregation.

Many congregations make the mistake of focusing on what they are *not* rather than what they *are*, what gifts they do *not* have, rather than how they *are* gifted. We can always develop new strengths and programs that amplify the ways in which we serve the community. Resist becoming immobilized because you see what you are *not* doing rather than becoming motivated to share the gifts you do have.

Recently Bill served a congregation that has the longest-running and most successful noon hour music concert series in North America. Nestled

---

13 An online spiritual gifts inventory is available from www.HealthierChurch.org

in uptown Waterloo, Ontario, this congregation is within blocks of two universities, and holds Tuesday noon hour concerts through the fall and winter that attract anywhere between 200 and 350 people.

The concerts are a huge success, and a significant outreach into the community. This congregation also has regular Out of the Cold dinners and sleepovers, and a variety of programs for children and youth. However, the noon hour concert series would not be in its thirty-sixth year if they had spent energy looking at this venture and said: "This is not a way to develop a small group ministry," or "This will not help young families face their growing economic pressures." No, a concert series does not do those things, but it does meet a need in the community, and does utilize strengths in the congregation and the community at large.

What can your congregation do, and how can it share its ministry? How can you use the gifts and skills of the community in which you find yourself? And once you have begun to implement one thing that gains traction and proves to be worthwhile, start something else that is new. Take one step at a time.

Finding a Beneficial Rhythm to Exercise Your Passions and Your Gifts

The Asian theologian Kosuke Koyama, in a helpful book *Three-mile-an-hour God,* reminds us that most people experience God in their daily lives as they walk about performing their daily tasks, rather than in specially organized activities and programs and events. Indeed, God goes with us–even when our journey is less than three miles an hour!

Let's connect the dots. On one end of the continuum is doing too much, and on the other end of the continuum is taking on more. How can you decide when you've taken on too much? Can you discern that, before you get seriously anxious? How can you know when you're not intentionally loafing? Can you discern that in order to know that it's time to take on something else?

When I was young, my parents told me, "Stay in your own yard." Don't go outside your yard. Think of your spiritual gifts as your yard. When you know your spiritual gifts, you will also learn when to say no to a request that is not consistent with your gifts.

On the other hand, how can you know when you could run faster? None of us performs up to capacity all the time. Think of your passion as a barometer that you can control in order to take advantage of the opportunities without overfunctioning.

It will be helpful for you to keep both your passion and your gifts in a rhythm and that will help you do what is beneficial to you, to your congregation, and to the kingdom of God.

Feel free to take on more. You also have permission to say no. Both are necessary wake-up calls for the congregation. Both are God-pleasing.

FOR FURTHER DISCUSSION

1. In what ways do you find it difficult to trust God fully? What do you need to help you trust in God more?
2. How does trusting in yourself both challenge and enable you to trust in God?
3. In what area of your life do you feel it's important for you to do more? In what area of your life to you feel it's important to do less? Why?
4. How do you earn the trust of others? How can you choose to trust someone that has not earned your trust?
5. Do you learn more by reading a book, tackling a project, or both equally? Give an example.

4

Transformational Hospitality

"I commend to you our sister Phoebe, a deacon of the church Cenchreae, so that you may welcome her in the yard, as is fitting for the saints, and help her in whatever she may require from you."[1]

A key principle of transformational leadership is that it will steadily move you toward some action and result. On the other hand, a key principle of transformational leadership is that it's based on listening, and listening occurs without an expectation for any result or action. It's plain to see that the principles of "asking" and "hospitality" are two very different principles of transformational leadership.

But, asking and hospitality are also two principles that must be blended into a unique combination that cannot be separated. If we separate them we invalidate both.

Hospitality means Listening

Hospitality must precede asking in order to legitimate the asking. In other words, it's important to listen before we speak if we expect some kind of transformation.

We usually consider our own congregation to be friendly, and that is often because most of us are friendly toward the people we know and with whom we associate. The bigger challenge is to be friendly to the guest in our midst, and even to the long-time member of the same congregation that we have simply never met. We are shocked to learn how many people in larger congregations attend the same house of

1 Romans 16:1-2.

worship for years yet do not know other regular attenders who sit just a few seats away.

Having said that, let's now parse both words with the hopeful result at the end of this chapter that we will be able to see holistic and wholesome transformational leadership.

Hospitality is one the most beautiful words in any language. Here is a starter kit for learning hospitality:

Hospitality initiates introducing yourself with an open hand to another in a way that creates a safe space for the other person to respond without fear. The mother of a young girl in worship noticed that her daughter was texting, and gently touched her arm and said, "Honey, we don't do that in church." Her daughter responded just as gently as she touched her mother's arm and said, "I am just sharing the peace with that Asian girl from school that is sitting across the aisle." Her mother responded, "I'm proud of you."

Hospitality enhances the dignity of the other person by respecting them, which suggests, "You matter to me." A wonderful example to show hospitality is noticing when the other person was not present and following up with some kind of contact. Some people react badly to the idea of "keeping weekly worship attendance," and it is not a custom as much as it used to be. Nonetheless most people like their absence and presence to be noticed.

I recently contacted a member who had been missing from all congregation events for over three months. I knew he had issues with some of our recent major decisions, both within the congregation and within the denomination, so I assumed he had taken time out to ponder these actions and his role in the congregation moving forward.

Ignoring his absence was not a helpful way to act, so as three months became four I made contact. I learned to my surprise he had significant health issues, that he was not mobile enough to come to worship, and that he was too unsteady to sit for an extended period of time in the upright pews. His absence was not a voluntary statement of disagreement on congregation policies, nor was it a protest on particular actions. He simply was unable to be present. In fact I learned that he wanted very much to be there.

We miss opportunities for connection with others by failing to notice when people are not present with us. It takes intentional sensitizing and caring to notice others' absence and presence. Risking saying, "I've missed seeing you. Have you been out of town?" seems worthwhile, as does remembering others in our prayers.

Hospitality identifies common interests, never differences. Just a caring, "How are things going?" can make a big difference in someone's life. It may be the only personal concern that that person has experienced all week.

Hospitality listens to the other person's stories. Again, just the simple question, "How are things going?" gives the person the opportunity to decline to share or a long-awaited opening with somebody who cared enough to listen.

Hospitality offers to walk together with the other person. Perhaps you can already see how this is transformational. This is the place to flesh out what you have discovered as a place where we can find some help together.

In an age of email communication, telephone messaging, and smart phone texting, it seems impossible to miss someone. Yet there are people who still do not have personal email accounts or a telephone messaging system. Those in nursing homes may be difficult to catch, with activities scheduled, family visits and outings, and necessary nap times at various periods in the day. So simply calling once and failing to make contact is not enough. We have to go the second mile and make a concerted effort to connect with others. The benefit is far greater than the effort needed to connect.

There may be no aspect of our faith that is more understated than that of hospitality. Patrick Keifert teaches the significance and underlying importance of hospitality.[2] We take exception to talk of "strangers" in worship, but hospitality is more than having someone over to your home for dinner or having greeters welcome people to worship.

Hospitality includes all forms of courtesy, etiquette, initiative, relationships, and evangelism. And it's all about listening.

---

2 Patrick Keifert, *Welcoming the Stranger.*

Asking Means Speaking

Asking is an equally beautiful word in any language. Asking is better than telling. Here is a starter kit for learning asking:

Asking begins with a genuine question. Be sure you really want to know the answer to the question you ask, and it will be a genuine question.

Asking connects both parties rather than separates them. You want to look for common interests, never differences. In fact, it's a rare situation when it's helpful to identify each other according to our differences.

Courtesy is not optional. This is so important that if someone makes a comment in public that is discourteous, such as, "Pastor doesn't care about our members, because he didn't visit our family member in the hospital," take it upon yourself to say, "I see it just the opposite way; Pastor visited my husband every week that he was in the hospital."

Asking is forthright and specific. General questions can actually sound insincere or create suspicion. "We'll have to get together sometime" is such an example. It would be much better to ask, "We would enjoy getting together with you; when would be a good date?"

Asking requests that the other person confirm our understanding of what they said. A simple, "I understood that you said...; did I hear you correctly?" Remember that the other person is the one who gets to decide whether we heard her correctly or not.

Let's take a humorous example of how listening and asking might fit together.

Combining Listening and Asking

The emphasis of the above sub-title is not on the gender reference, but to reframe the stereotype a little differently than we might have imagined. If you're male: Have you ever been out driving and not known what direction to take? Have you ever driven somewhere in your car and found yourself in strange territory? How did you handle these dilemmas? Did you ask any female in the car for their opinion?

At the risk of oversimplifying the profundity of being lost, it is appealing to suggest the simplest of all ways to resolve this complex issue: Ask. The gender jokes suggest that this tendency does not occur in females. They simply find someone to ask. The male of the species, it is suggested, is simply too proud to ask someone else for directions. It is probably accurate to say that there is a certain bravado that is culturally ingrained in the male psyche, but it is equally plausible that resisting asking directions is a matter of pride, regardless of gender. There you have it. Another myth busted. But this tendency may stem from something much deeper than simply asking for directions. The punch line is simply that the failure in this story might not have only been a resistance to asking, but it could also have been caused by not listening to the female's opinion.

"Ask" is a one-word transformational principle—so simple and so profound. Jesus says, "Ask, and it shall be given unto you." As my mentor said, "That's worth looking into."[3] It is that simple, and that profound. But the guy says, "You work where I work, you get home, get a bite to eat, watch a little TV; you can't just be asking, asking, asking." Good worker, hard worker, sincere. But you've got to be more than a good worker. You've got to be a good asker. "Ask!" That's worth looking into.

Miroslav Volf provides the global solution for this malady in the bluntest possible wording.[4] He insists that it is only the unconditional love of God in Jesus Christ that can free us from the bondage of pride and works righteousness. Let go of everything that bothers you. Let go of your pride, your tendency to justify yourself, your egocentric need to justify, and then fill that empty spot in your life with God's grace. Volf suggests that everything in our society that is dysfunctional can only be resolved by leaning on the everlasting arms of God.

This is a classic description of the central doctrine of the Christian faith. It is also counter-intuitive. We tend to want to do things our own way.

Go the second mile, beyond one email or phone call

One needs to make a concerted effort to connect with others. The benefit is far greater than the effort needed to connect.

3 Jim Rohn, who regularly made profound suggestions by understating the obvious.

4 Miroslav Volf, *Free of Charge: Giving and Forgiving in a Culture Stripped of Grace.*

Ed says that one of his favorite activities in a congregation was to take the Lord's Supper to a shut-in or homebound person. So often, the visit would end with a homebound person saying, "Thank you so much for coming. You're the only person I have seen this week."

Follow Up!

Many ministers openly say they see no purpose in visiting. "Why should I bother lining up visits with people with whom I must drink tea and eat cookies? It is hard enough to remain healthy and watch one's weight in this profession."

It is always good to connect with people in the congregation or who share in the ministry of the congregation. You have an immediate way to develop rapport with the person by thanking them for what they are doing and expanding God's mission.

It is also easier subsequently to visit people and request support for an activity if you have previously made a visit simply to get to know the person. The best way to avoid the criticism "the church only calls on me when they want something or they are looking for money" is to make sure a visitation team keeps regular contact throughout the year.

One of our favorite habits is to contact someone we haven't seen for quite a while, and say, "I haven't seen you for quite a while. How about if we get together for lemonade?" Those occasions often turn into some of our favorite experiences in congregations.

Of course, the easiest of all opportunities to connect is to not hurry out the door after worship, but just take a minute to notice someone who's off in a corner by herself and offer her a friendly greeting. It did not cost you more than the breath to blow out a candle, but think how important it might be to her.

Say "Thank You" Every Chance You Get

One of the basic characteristics of a thriving congregation is that every one in leadership in such churches has a habit of saying, "Thank you." We do that very poorly in our congregations—at least in Canada, but likely elsewhere too.

Bill is a former Executive Minister of Financial Stewardship for the United Church, and one year he travelled extensively throughout the country, making donations during those travels (where he often spoke at a congregation's worship service) to nine different congregations.

At the end of the year he received receipts from all nine congregations. Most had simply sent the required signed receipt with the government charitable registration number on it. That's understandable.

For example, one receipt was printed at the top and a general "Thank you for your gift" statement at the bottom. No receipt was personally acknowledged with a hand-written note. Some of these gifts were a one-time donation; others were the result of monthly visits, and so came to a significant amount by the end of the year. In all cases, the receipt implied that the gifts were more expected than appreciated.

It can often be a challenge to get congregations to say "thanks" personally and regularly. We assume people "should give." The reality is there are many options for one's gift—over 85,000 charities in Canada alone—and so refusing to show thanks can often be detrimental to the well-being of the faith community.

But saying "thanks" does not always need to be related to money. Someone does an extra few hours of gardening at the church. Another helps paint a Sunday school room. Still another repairs a leaking toilet, and yet another reads scripture for worship. "The flower garden really looks nice." "You really brightened up the Sunday school room." "Thank you so much for fixing that leak. We really needed it." "As far as I'm concerned, you can read the Bible lesson any Sunday that I'm in worship." It's really quite simple to acknowledge what someone else has done, without being effusive.

I offer a new idea: why not write a letter of thanks after visiting a congregational member? Pastors may think they are the ones who deserve the thanks for caring enough to visit, but such a note of appreciation sends a clear message of hospitality to a congregational participant when you write, "Thank you for welcoming me into your home and for sharing in a wonderful visit that has bolstered my spirit simply because you gave me the special opportunity to be in your presence." People feel welcomed and important when they are thanked for being a part of the congregation.

Danny Meyer offers ways that his own experience in the restaurant business has helped him to understand hospitality as a powerful business principle.[5] Without altering his approach and insights, one could equally see the book as offering help in discerning the transforming power of hospitality in the congregation, though that was not his intent when he wrote the book. Meyer is so convinced that hospitality is essential in any business transaction that he says "Virtually nothing else is as important as how one is made to feel in any business transaction."[6]

Could we not say the same of Jesus' interactions with every person he healed? "Neither do I condemn you. Go and sin no more."[7] Hospitality is not a new concept. It is an essential part of living and sharing the gospel. "Be ready with a meal or a bed when it's needed. This way, some have extended hospitality to strangers without ever knowing it."[8]

Often we want people to fit our needs, while what we should do is accept them for who they are and for what they can offer. It is not only a message of giving, but also courteous receiving, which sometimes may be more difficult. Are we ready to accept the generous, unencumbered gifts that come our way?

That's what it means to go the second mile. "Don't hit back at all. If someone strikes you, stand there and take it. If someone drags you into court and sues for the shirt off your back, giftwrap your best coat to make a present of it. And if someone takes unfair advantage of you, use the occasion to practice the servant life, no more tit for tat stuff. Live generously."[9]

Welcome the Unexpected Guest

One evening while leading worship at an aboriginal congregation north of where he lived, Bill noticed a woman enter while the service was underway. She came forward at the offering time and said that God put it in her heart that she was to come and sing for the congregation that evening. She offered

---

5 Danny Meyer, *The Transforming Power of Hospitality in Business.*
6 Ibid., p.11.
7 John 8:11.
8 Hebrews 13:2 Eugene Peterson, *The Message.*
9 Matthew 5:40–42.

her gift of song, and was gone within fifteen minutes, perhaps to another worship gathering. The people in the community accepted the gift as any gift should be accepted: freely given, freely received.

That experience was unlike anything Bill had experienced in the many non-aboriginal congregations he had served in the twenty previous years. He was used to worship being scripted, tightly arranged, and rigorously organized. Nothing would go off the rail thanks to hours of planning—at least that was the intent. Yet when we organize our congregational worship experiences in such a tight manner we are no longer open to the gifts of the spirit that may come our way, and are poorer for it.

Recently I asked my children what was an important Christmas tradition for them in their growing up years. I expected it would be the outside light display we had, as we were opposite the largest light display in the town, so we needed to decorate our home somewhat to complement the display across the road. Or maybe they were impressed by the lovely gift baskets we received from generous local farmers and orchard owners. Or maybe they remembered the family tradition of allowing them to open one gift on Christmas Eve after the family worship service. Surely that was a highlight. Then again, watching the family favorite movie "A Christmas Story" in its original VCR format must be on the list of highlights, I thought; after all, watching it is still a Christmas Day ritual.

It was none of the above. My older daughter spoke up right away when asked what the highlight of Christmas had been to her growing up. "It was the fact we never knew who would be at our table for Christmas, because Dad often found someone who needed a meal and had no home or family with whom to share Christmas. I learned so much every year from these interesting people." What at the time seemed almost scary and foolish on my part, bringing people I barely knew into the family home with young children, became a highlight for them.

When we move beyond our comfortable routines, growth happens. The common definition of insanity is "doing the same thing over and over and over again and expecting a different result." Is that the trap many of our congregations are in these days? We are so sure we know what the business of the congregation is, and how we should conduct ourselves. We feel threatened and vulnerable and so feel the need to protect our traditions. But should we? Often the traditions we protect are habits and rituals that serve us, but that do not allow us to serve the gospel.

Now such a response to the unexpected is understandable. Jesus was taken aback when a woman touched the edge of his clothing. "Who touched me?" he asked, probably not in a dispassionate way, either. Jesus quickly learned that those chance encounters, and random contacts, often formed the most significant moments of his ministry. If we can be blessed and transformed by some of the random acts of kindness into which we are drawn, we will be better Christians for it.

When we get caught up in worrying about our congregation's finances, we will never find ways to be genuinely hospitable. Stories abound of instances of hospitality across the mid-west of this continent during the redistribution of the population from the east to the west. In the 1920s and '30s many people travelled west on cargo trains and boxcars, seeking a new beginning. In pursuit of a dream, they often found life in the west even more difficult than what they had left behind. Yet people kept coming west, and often those who were already settled in the west, struggling for a living, fed those unexpected guests as best they could. Unexpected guests, but not unwelcomed guests. Hospitality was lived and shared.

Growing up we all knew where we could land for dinner, uninvited. We knew the friends who liked to have someone come over for dinner, and the mothers and fathers who welcomed us into their homes. Often these were not the wealthy families of the neighborhood, or even the fairly well-off families within the working-class neighborhood of our origins. With a little creativity such families could make a dinner for four or five feed a gathering of six. No one went hungry, and most importantly, everyone felt welcomed and a part of the family for that meal.

Who is Really Welcome in Your Congregation?

Is your congregation that kind of welcoming place? Bill tells the story, now with a smile, of how his Doctor of Ministry supervisor arrived for worship at the congregation he was then serving to get a sense of the community of faith. No sooner had the professor found a seat in what he thought was a safe pew, about four rows from the back and near the side of the sanctuary (after all, he did not want to take someone's treasured spot), when a ninety-year-old member came along and told him in a suitably indignant tone of voice: "You are sitting in my seat and so you must move over." The professor took this reprimand with good humor.

Imagine, however, if it had been a newcomer looking for a sense of community, a safe place to share one's spiritual yearning, or simply wanting to spend some quiet time in prayer before worship started. Would a newcomer be so willing to be amused at the experience? Isn't the whole purpose of the congregation to be aware of and sensitive to the needs of others? How far does your congregation go to be clear about its purpose, its orientation to others, and its call to share the gospel with a sense of justice and with love? Are you hospitable, making room for others, or are you a congregation filled with people who live their purpose through making sure they are "Keepers of the Seat"?

In conclusion, the possibility of transformational leadership cannot occur without hospitality as a listening lifestyle. Hospitality is meeting the other person's needs, whether they are simply being welcomed for showing up or are spending an entire evening with you.

Hospitality is seeing with our ears and listening with our eyes. Hospitality is noticing. Hospitality is seeing behind the silence, and being enriched by knowing what's going on in another person's life.

Hospitality is specifically mentioned as a spiritual gift in the Scripture.[10] It is significant. It is easy to see why hospitality would be a prerequisite for transformational leadership.

However, intentional asking is also a prerequisite for transformational leadership. Again, it is not possible to appropriately and intentionally ask unless the "ask" has been preceded by intentional listening. Stewardship leaders by and large agree that the primary reason that people do not increase their giving is because they haven't been asked. A pastor friend of Ed's complained that one of the members of his congregation gave $50,000 to the Rotary Camp instead of giving it to the church. Ed asked, "Why did

10 The references to hospitality occur very prominently in Romans chapters 12 and 13, 1 Peter chapter 4, and 1 Timothy chapter 3.

he do that?" The pastor said, "I don't know." Ed replied, "Why don't you ask him?" The pastor was hesitant to talk about stewardship, but he agreed. The congregation member said that he didn't give it to the church "because no one asked me." Development officers agree completely with this principle. Scripture is replete with examples of intentional asking,[11] even to the extent of warning us, "you do not have, because you do not ask."[12] Jesus' example of hospitality is that he actually went out the synagogue doors and into the places where people need hospitality. Go into those places.[13]

Transformational leadership through invitational hospitality is simple, and in fact, we all know how to do it without needing certification. It is like companionship. We all know how to be someone's companion. That is a wake-up call for some congregations. And it is God-pleasing.

FOR FURTHER DISCUSSION

1. How big is God's promise in that one little word "ask" in "ask and you shall receive," and how do you imagine God might limit himself in fulfilling that promise?
2. When is it important to take the initiative to introduce yourself to a stranger?
3. Which principle of hospitality stands out as most important to you? Why?
4. How would you know if you were really welcome in a congregation?

11 We are commanded to ask God for his counsel (Judges 18:5); and to ask in prayer (Matthew 21:22); and people who have been given greater capacity will be asked to accept greater responsibility (Luke 12:48); and of course the familiar saying "Ask and you shall receive" (John 16:24).

12 James 4:2.

13 Matthew 25.

5

Choosing How to Carry Our Rocks

"Bear one another's burdens, and in this way you will fulfill the law of Christ...."For all must carry their own loads.""[1]

Each of Us Carries a Unique Bag of Rocks

Imagine for just a moment that we were each born with what we might call "a bag of rocks," rocks that represent what is unchangeable. Such obvious things as our height, for example. Ed laughingly says, "When I was a child, I really wanted to be 6'11" tall and play professional basketball. I don't think I'm going to make it. I've grown as much as I can grow; and there is also the matter of not having that much athletic capacity."

Like Ed's height, our physical and mental capacities also have some developmental boundaries. Our racial composition and ethnicity is beyond our control. Those things are simply rocks we carry. Like months of the calendar, we adjust to these facts, choose our attitude. You may not like January, but it exists whether or not you tear that page off the calendar.

Three oft-neglected rocks are our feelings, thoughts, and actions. We were all born with the capacity to carry those three rocks transformationally by handling them in a healthy way. There may have been times when we blamed others, complained, or felt sorry for ourselves, but those would be unhealthy ways of dealing with our feelings, thoughts, and actions. The fact is that we can choose how we respond to life.

1 Galatians 6:2 & 6:5

Carry Your Own Rocks

Picture yourself being born with a bag of rocks that you are to carry all your life. What's the first thing you think about when carrying a bag of rocks? That it's heavy? That it's more than you can handle? Or do you think of the possibility that you might be carrying treasure? Or that you could use the rocks to begin to build a path or a dwelling?

At certain times you may see your rocks as life-giving, and at other times you may see your rocks as being life-draining. The fact is that all rocks can be both. If you go rock climbing, the rocks both provide a solid footing and might prompt you to fall. Bill tells of his recent camp experience in northern Ontario. Each year he looks forward to a couple of weeks in the bush of Algoma District on an island in the northern channel of Lake Huron. The main activities he'd set for himself this year were painting a set of wired furniture for the deck outside his trailer, and expanding trails that surround his campsite. As usual, he also took time to gaze at the changing natural beauty of the pond there, including the turtles that sun themselves on a log.

This year, however, when he looked out to where the floating log had always welcomed the turtles, there were no turtles. The Ministry of Transportation had sent in a backhoe a couple of years earlier and removed part of the beaver dam that created the pond, fearing it may give way and wash out the highway some 150 feet away. Consequently, the log on which the turtles had typically sunned themselves, instead of sitting in several feet of water, was now mired in mud punctuated by a few small puddles of water. It was a disheartening part of Bill's holidays, and like a child picking a scab on an old wound, he found himself looking once or twice every day at that log, hoping the world would right itself and the turtles would magically appear. They never did.

It reminded him of a similar experience over twenty-five years earlier, when suddenly the frogs living in the pond had disappeared. To be fair, the Steadman family often was kept awake at night by the croaking of the frogs when the trailer windows were wide open to the breeze, and despite the fun the children had catching the occasional frog, the nighttime chorus often made them wish the frogs would go away or be quiet. When they did go away as part of a huge reduction of frogs across North America in the late 1900s, the silence was deafening. What a loss.

It was not much fun to miss the frogs in an earlier time, or the turtles on this occasion. So it was with excitement that later in his week at camp Bill walked up past the old pond site now turned into marshy, reedy grassland, and saw that the secondary beaver dam, a few hundred feet from the roadway, remained intact. There was still a significant amount of water in this section of the pond that was located further upstream.

As Bill gathered some of the beaver-cut poles on the edge of the dam for burning and for using as walking sticks, and as he removed some wooden poles within the dam itself to free water to flow into the lower pond area, he noticed an amazing sight—a log with four or five turtles on it. The turtles were gathered together on this fallen log like buddies standing around a bar discussing the weekly NFL scores.

When Bill changed his perspective, he realized that the turtles had not left: they had moved. And they moved not necessarily because they wanted to, but in response to their changed environment. The pond had as it were abandoned them, so the turtles moved to another spot that met their needs.

So it is with our experiences within our congregations. People are not so much abandoning the congregation as an institution as finding a new congregation to meet their needs when they feel their local congregation has abandoned them. It behooves us to consider why. And that sometimes takes a change in the way we look at things.

Which of Your Rocks are Stepping Stones?

What was most transformational for me was this threefold category called "feelings, thoughts, and actions."

When I was young and immature, I blamed others. I became very good at it. In particular I blamed others for the fact that I didn't look good. I blamed my parents. I blamed my boss. I blamed the government. I blamed the church. I blamed God. I blamed my lousy neighbors for not being willing to loan me money. My mentor taught me in the very blunt way that I needed: "Big problem with your list of people to blame, Ed: you aren't on it!"

That was a transformational learning for me. I can point to that day as one that turned my life around. It happened as I came to understand more about God's design for my life. My rocks became stepping stones.

Transformational leaders find a way to see the value in those around them, and encourage people at any age and stage of life to develop their strengths of leadership. Bill was asked as a university student to be an advisor to the then premier of Ontario, William G. Davis. He had a couple of audiences with the premier, but mainly spoke with advisors and aides about issues that were important to university students in Ontario in the early 1970s.

Recently he had an opportunity to speak with Bill Davis at a large fundraising dinner, and he offered a "thank you" to the former Premier for his kind acceptance of him as a young university student in his office. "You always treated me with respect, as if I was an equal," remarked Steadman. The former Premier, in a voice retained for serious and important observations, responded: "That was easy, because you are."

Transformational leaders see the value in what others bring. They look beyond what might be inexperience, or immature opinions and ideas, or lack of knowledge, and lift up the gifts that these other individuals bring. Transformational leaders surround themselves with strong, able people. Why? Because they know that strong people can only enhance their ability and aid their understanding and knowledge of any particular issue. It is weak people who surround themselves with weak people, for they feel threatened by someone with skills and gifts.

Look at the disciples Jesus chose—they were hardly weak people. They were feisty, determined, committed, and passionate. They may have been an unpredictable lot at times, but Jesus must have known that. He chose them for who they were and what they could be. Jesus saw the up side in others, and calls us to do the same.

Transformational leaders bring down barriers. They open doors, and welcome dialogue. They see opportunity where others may see challenges. The only way to find helpful answers is to ask (or welcome) difficult questions.

There are certain rocks in your rock bag that give you the possibility of overcoming any obstacle, while at the same time presenting the danger of preventing you from reaching any dream or goal in life. Listen to this next sentence; it is transformational.

You are already the recipient of the greatest career, the greatest future you will ever have. You are the life-long "Director of Your Feelings, Thoughts, and Actions." No one can take this career from you without your permission. No one can fire you, downsize you, or terminate you. Accepting this position automatically makes you a transformational leader. Even if you would like a position with more responsibility, you need to know that this is as good as it gets. Accept the offer of being in charge of your own feelings, thoughts, and actions. Take advantage of this promotion right now and it is yours.

Your rocks are your God-given opportunity to be a transformational leader. However, they also reveal your greatest threat, humanly speaking. All you are asked to do is carry your bag of rocks. In other words, be responsible for every feeling you have. Be responsible for every thought you think. Be responsible for every action you take. It's that simple, and that difficult.

What Does it Look Like To Carry Your Own Rocks?

If you take responsibility for your feelings, your life will be forever blame-free. Every feeling you experience is within your power to manage. I automatically get the ability to manage any feeling simply by accepting responsibility for it.

What a difference it makes when we stop using language such as "You make me angry" or "Your attitude is getting on my nerves" that blames others, and instead clarify how we feel, through such observations as, "I feel anxious when things are not well planned," and "I do not feel comfortable or know how to approach you when you are emotionally agitated." Owning our own feelings, emotions, and uncertainties is far more healthy, helpful, and possible than trying to manage the feelings and emotions of others.

Since the late 1980s much work has been done on the issue of Emotional Intelligence. Daniel Goldman's seminal work on this topic has encouraged other studies on how our emotional maturity helps us to be successful and proficient in life. One statistic that surprised us, products as we are of the importance of having a learned clergy, is that only 20% of people with a high I.Q. and a low score on Emotional Intelligence are successful in their career choices and life activities, whereas 80% who score high in Emotional Intelligence but who have average intelligence, are successful. Why is that? Much of life is built upon our relationships with others, or our ability to work effectively with others. We need more than intellectual gifts; we need to be mature in our own emotional make-up and sensitive to the emotional needs of others.

You are the director of whether or not you feel happy, content, grateful, generous, caring, confident, courageous, and so on. You are also the director of whether or not you feel resentful, stingy, critical, afraid, selfish, dissatisfied, sad, and a literally unlimited number of other feelings.

I used to look forward to when things changed. I learned that "things change when you change." I learned that I was in charge of whether or not I chose to be upset. If I get upset, whose rock is it? If I blame others for upsetting me, I am doing nothing less than relinquishing the power to upset me. Whose rock is that? It is my rock. I can choose to be calm. I can choose not to be upset by anything that happens. I am the director of whether or not I get upset. Is it my imagination, or do people in congregations seem to allow themselves to get upset more than the general population? If so, why do you think that is? More important, we can do something about it. We can take charge of our emotions, and by doing so we will impact the emotions expressed within our various congregations.

If we keep the image of the bag of rocks that we carry, blaming others is like trying to take a rock out of my bag and putting it into the other person's bag. If someone else gets offended at something I say or do, whose rock is that? Why would anyone want to take a rock out of their bag and put it in someone else's bag? Any time you fail to carry your rock of how you feel you set yourself up to be handcuffed and/or manipulated by others.

Transformational leaders help everyone be responsible for their own feelings, thoughts, and actions. Please say, "I am responsible for my own feelings, thoughts, and actions. No one else is." Now, please say, "Others are responsible for their own actions, not I." That does not mean that we can trade in our "freedom of speech" for "a license to say anything we want." It does mean, though, that in order to be a follower of Jesus, in order to be a transformational leader, we are free to be responsible for our feelings, thoughts, and actions, and we are also free from abusing that gift of God.

A transformational leader is not afraid of what others might say. S/he is not bothered by criticism. The apostle Paul says, "Each of us must bear our own burden."[2] Carry your own rocks. For example, my wife and I made a commitment to go to an event, which, upon reflection, had

2 Galatians 5:1–10.

become inconvenient for me. In our heart of hearts we knew that the other would likely be disappointed if one of us dropped out. I have the primary responsibility to express my need, and my wife has the primary responsibility for expressing how that affects her needs.

On the other hand, I also have a primary responsibility to express my needs in a caring and gentle way. "Bear one another's burdens."[3] Jesus said, "Go the second mile." Carry your own rocks (feelings, thoughts, and actions), and also help others carry their rocks, yet without shouldering the primary responsibility for them (or their feelings, thoughts, and actions). I can do exactly that by patiently listening, not rushing to a decision, and by asking my wife to clarify anything I do not fully understand. She can do the same. Note that this "tactic" does not mean that I will "get my way." It could, in fact, result in my needing to accept being uncomfortable with my momentary inconvenience "this time," or in a modified way, or with any of a variety of choices that emerge out of our engaging each other.

The underlying God-given transformational reality is that my wife and my relationship with her is more important than the differences we will encounter. To put it another way, we discuss any inconvenience that is important to either of us. Sometimes one of us lives with the inconvenience, sometimes the other lives with it. And neither of us keeps score, except to ask, "How did it go for you?" after the fact. Our relationship grows as a result, and our transformational leadership ability soars, for we have taken ownership of our own feelings while making room for trying to appreciate and respond to the feelings of the other.

Now, transfer this transformational principle to your relationship with your congregation. What would your congregation look like if everyone took primary responsibility for carrying their own rock bag? What difference would it make in your life together and in your life as a follower of Jesus and how would it impact your congregation's mission to reconcile the world if we would each take primary responsibility for our own feelings, thoughts, and actions? It would make all the difference in the world.

Take, for example, the people in the congregation who are uninvolved, under-involved, and uninvited. (And if you don't like that label, that's

3 Ibid.

fine. Just think of the large percentage of the congregation who does not participate in the ministries of the congregation in carrying out God's mission.) This may be our greatest wake-up call as a congregation. If only there were a way that we could engage the uninvolved, the under-involved, and the unclaimed in our congregation.

There *is* a way to engage inactive members: Show interest in their lives and they will show renewed interest in the congregation.

One successful congregation has a bulletin board on which they post all of the activities of congregants that are recorded in the local newspaper. Even the Sunday hockey games played by children who no longer come to Sunday school have a place of prominence. Some people thought advertising hockey games that are played on a Sunday morning was not the way to encourage attendance in worship. But the pastor insisted that the congregation show care for all of the people in that community of faith, even for those that are unable to be present each week.

What was the result? The congregation made time each week to celebrate others' successes, and many of those who are absent in winter during hockey season, or others who are away in summer during baseball season, make a point of reconnecting when they are able to come on Sundays, because they know the community cares for them as individuals. The congregation has not lowered its standards of what is expected from its members; they have reconnected to become more truly the people of God in that community.

If we would do the same, the turnaround in our congregations would be immense. The possibilities would be endless. The trends of decline would be reversed. Most important, God's mission to reconcile the world would be enhanced by our modeling reconciliation and mutual support within our own community of faith.

Transformational Leaders Read, Listen, and Watch

I was fortunate to sit at the feet of a wise man who became my mentor.[4] He taught me the importance of carrying my own rock bag, and he pushed me to grow and become able to teach others to do the same.

4 Jim Rohn.

As soon as I was ready to accept my responsibility for my own feelings, thoughts and actions, my mentor taught me some basic principles of how we humans can be transformed by how we read, listen, and watch. He told this story:

A business owner took one of her managers to lunch, and asked, "Do you like your work?" He said, "Sure." "May I ask you why you aren't doing better than you used to do?" Excellent question! He replied, "I'm a good worker, hard worker, sincere." The business owner said, "You're right. You are a good worker, hard worker, sincere. What are you reading?" The employee replied, "You know what it's like to work here. When you get home, you've got to get a bite to eat, watch a little TV, and go to bed. You can't be reading, reading, reading." And the guy is behind on his car payment! She said, "You've got to be more than a good worker, hard worker, sincere. You've got to be a good reader."

Then she asked, "What did you hear when you listened at the last meeting?" He replied, "You know what it's like to work here. When you get home, you've got to get a bite to eat, watch a little TV, and it's time to go to bed. You can't be listening, listening, listening." And the guy is behind on his car payment. You've got to be more than a good worker, hard worker, sincere. You've got to be a good listener.

She asked, "What have you noticed from watching the other people that work here? He replied, "You know what it's like to work here. When you get home, you've got to get a bite to eat, watch a little TV, and it's time to go to bed. You can't be watching, watching, watching." And the guy is behind on his car payment. You've got to be more than a good worker, hard worker, sincere. You need to be a good watcher.

Those same principles apply to our life within our congregations. The pastor took his leadership team leader to lunch and asked, "Do you like your work?" They said, "Sure. We are good workers, hard workers, sincere." The pastor asked, "What are you reading?" The stewardship team leader replied, "You work where I work, when you get home, you've got to get a bite to eat, watch a little TV, it's time to go to bed. You can't be reading, reading, reading." And the stewardship leader is behind on his stewardship planning! "You've got to be more than a good worker, hard worker, sincere. You got to be a good reader."

Then the pastor asked, "What did you hear when you listened at the last council meeting?" He replied, "You work where I work, when you get home, you've got to get a bite to eat, watch a little TV, and it's time to go to bed. You can't be listening, listening, listening." And the stewardship leader is behind on his stewardship planning. You've got to be more than a good worker, hard worker, sincere. You've got to be a good listener."

The pastor asked, "What have you noticed from watching the other team leaders?" He replied, "You work where I work, when you get home, you've got to get a bite to eat, watch a little TV, and it's time to go to bed. You can't be watching, watching, watching." And the stewardship leader is behind on making his contacts.

These principles also apply to leadership within the regions or judicatories of our various denominations. A Bishop took some pastors to lunch and asked, "Do you like your ministry?" The pastors replied, "We are good workers, hard workers, sincere." The Bishop asked, "What are you reading? "What did you hear when you listened at the last pastors' conference?" "What have you noticed from observing other pastors?" You've got to be more than good workers, hard workers, sincere. You've got to be good readers, listeners, and observers."

Jesus invited the whole congregation to a meal at the altar, and asked, "Do you like being my followers?" And they replied, "We're good workers, hard workers, sincere." Jesus asked them, "What are you reading? What did you get out of listening to the last worship service? Who did you observe was not there? Whom have you invited to take a spiritual gifts inventory?" They all replied, "You know what it's like with our busy schedules. We are good workers, hard workers, sincere. You do what we do, when we get home, we've got to get a bite to eat, watch a little TV, and it's time to go to bed. We can't spend all our time reading, listening, observing who isn't there, and inviting, inviting, and inviting." And the congregation is behind. Congregations have to be more than good workers, hard workers, sincere. They need to be good observers and inviters. "Bring in the crippled and the lame."[5] Whatever their needs are, meet them. Be transformational leaders.

5 Luke 14:13.

Transformational Leaders Judge No One

But there is more. The next principle is to judge no one. Many people find this a difficult principle to understand. Why do we have the urge to judge others? What do we not understand about God's message in the Scriptures, "Do not judge, or you too will be judged"? Jesus' warning is clear: "The same way you judge others, you will be judged." And then Jesus gets even more specific: "And with the measure you use, it will be measured to you."[6]

What do we not understand about the biblical messages about money? We don't argue with people about anything, especially not stewardship, whether it's about giving our time, or our talent, or our treasure to God's work. We simply invite them to read these clear words and answer what God is calling them to do. And instead of responding to God's call, they often look for the exceptions or think up excuses. And they mistakenly think that they will feel better if they compare themselves to others...judge them...exclude them...discount them.

Judging ourselves has got to go too. St. Paul says, "I do not even judge myself."[7]

What is transformational about this? It is that we have immediate access to God's grace in Jesus Christ, through the Holy Spirit. Wake up, follower of Jesus. No matter what you have done in the past, no matter how terrible the past chapters of your life, God's good news in Jesus Christ is that each of us has already been forgiven for all of that, and each of us has already been empowered to write the next chapter in the book of our lives. The Holy Spirit has found a place to live in our hearts and already makes us able to make wise choices as we grow stronger day by day, by carrying our rocks in healthy ways.

Wake up, congregation. No matter what you have done in the past, no matter how terrible the past chapters of your congregation have been, God's good news in Jesus Christ is that all who are connected with our congregation in any way have already been forgiven for all that we have failed to do. God's good news is that we have already been empowered to write the next chapter in the book of our congregation as we discern ways

6 Matthew 7:1.
7 2 Corinthians 4:3.

that God wants us to expand God's mission. The Holy Spirit has already empowered us to make wise choices as we grow stronger day by day in healthy ways. That is transformational. And it is God-pleasing.

FOR FURTHER DISCUSSION

1. How do the lessons learned from turtles and frogs relate to your congregation's a) current, and b) future situation?
2. Describe one of your rocks and the potential stepping stone you see in it.
3. According to the authors, you are the director of whether or not you feel happy, content, grateful, generous, caring, confident, and courageous. Do you believe this? Do you really believe this? Describe an experience from your life to document your answer.
4. The authors also say, "You are also the director of whether or not you feel resentful, stingy, critical, afraid, selfish, dissatisfied, and sad." How is this different or similar to the choices in question #3? Which of the two is most difficult for you to manage? Why do you suppose that is?
5. Is it my imagination, or do people in congregations seem to allow themselves to get upset more than the general population? If so, why do you think that is? What can you personally do about that?

6

Reinventing Your Vision of Living the Gospel with Hope

"Now faith is the assurance of things hoped for, the conviction of things not seen... By faith we understand that the worlds were prepared by the word of God, so that what is seen was made from things that are not visible."[1]

Living the gospel of Jesus Christ is more than attending church, hearing a few sermons, or entering into a discussion group. It is more than being involved in a small group or helping at an outreach ministry. Living the gospel of Jesus Christ impacts everything we do and say, think and feel.

That may be difficult to understand, much less integrate into our lives, for much of what we do today is compartmentalized. Rarely do we know people in all of the facets of their existence. We have work colleagues and then we have residents in our neighborhood; we have fellow church members and we have people we know from the gym or favorite sports venues. Even our families may be so spread out that we do not know well our own cousins or newly-born grandchildren if they live half way across the globe. How can we expect people in our congregation to know all about our lives, much less be clear about the values that are important to us?

How we live our lives, set our priorities, and pursue our goals should be based on our integration of the gospel message into our entire lives. There should be no significant difference in the way in which we live and

1 Hebrews 11:1, 3.

act as followers of Jesus in different contexts—in the local congregation or wider judicatory, in the grocery store line or behind the steering wheel of our car, at our job or with our family or chatting with our neighbors. If we approach life filled with the gospel message, we need not worry about where we are because we have already determined how we will act.

Members and Guests Are All the Same in God's Eyes

If we act consistently in response to the impact of the gospel on our lives, then we should not treat people any differently either. Whether a person is a first-time attender to your congregation or the largest financial contributor and most committed participant in your congregation, they deserve to be treated with respect, concern, and a warm welcome. Those pastors who are excellent at providing pastoral care have no more time and often no greater counselling skills than other pastors. What they are adept at doing is making people feel important. They let those that they are visiting know that they have their undivided attention during any visit or personal interaction.

Congregations often think they are welcoming and friendly, but the truth is that often people are welcoming and friendly only with the folk they already know. It is essential that all who enter the doors of a congregation or have some interaction with a community of faith sense that the welcome mat has been put out for them. Wherever we are and whatever we are doing, we want to help others feel welcomed and important—important to us, but even more significantly, important to God.

How the Vision of the Gospel May be Lost

Sometimes a congregation can't avoid slipping back, or backsliding. Do you know how to tell when a congregation starts going downhill, when it has lost the true sense of how to live the Gospel message? A congregation skid begins the day it decides to take a percentage of offerings away from people in poverty, or in hunger, or from partners in mission so they can "have enough" for themselves.[2]

2 Matthew 25:3–45.

That message is perceived by congregation leaders as being a "stewardship problem," aka, "We don't have enough money." So they think that if they publicize the message, "If everyone increases their giving $5.00 a week..." that will solve the stewardship problem. And they are disappointed when their request is not enthusiastically welcomed. One person says, "I can't give any more." Another says, ""We can barely make ends meet as it is." In my case, I said to the congregation leaders, "You know that we will be cutting back our giving because my wife retired and we went from two incomes to one income..."

Of course there are congregation situations when financial setbacks create unavoidable cash flow problems, but "not having enough money" is not a "stewardship problem." It signals a failure to re-invent your vision of living the gospel with hope.

When Our Income Decreases

Ed shares this story from his personal life:

Our congregation was wisely conducting its annual stewardship response, called Commitment Sunday. It was well done. My wife and I were not made to feel guilty. The financial need was great. We wanted to give more, even while going from two incomes to one income.

But after my wife closed our health care business in Kansas City, and with it the loss of a job, she moved to Chicago to be with me, and we said "we can get by." But the financial bottom fell out from under us. Our lives changed suddenly when sixty-five positions were eliminated where I worked, and mine was one of them. We were shocked and saw little hope for how we were going to live. We had now gone from two incomes to zero incomes.

After many conversations, and sufficient time to pray and think, surprisingly, we didn't struggle as much as we had when we went from two incomes to one income. We simply increased our giving 1%. We reasoned, "If we trust in God, and if there will be no additional income in the future, 1% of zero is zero, then whether we give more money to God's work is just as much God's problem." So it was actually quite easy to trust in God, in that situation. You might say that we "re-invented our vision of living the gospel with hope."

While working in the General Council office of The United Church of Canada, Bill helped to facilitate an investment from a rural congregation that had received a donation of $50,000 from a deceased member. The annual interest from that fund would go to the Mission and Service Fund (the church's fund for ministry and mission at the national level). The congregation wanted the money to be invested through The United Church of Canada Foundation, allowing the interest to be paid automatically every year. Since the minimum amount for separate fund investments was $50,000, the commitment could easily be handled.

But there was another story to this investment. Fifteen years earlier Bill had been a Stewardship Consultant in the presbytery that included this particular congregation. One cold November evening he met with the Finance Committee of that congregation, and the chair of the committee announced, with no hesitation and almost some pride, that because the church was in financial need, it had stopped promoting the Mission and Service Fund, and was asking people to donate money to the local congregation instead, so that a badly needed new furnace could be purchased.

Speaking as much from the heart as from a proper statistical analysis of the congregation, I had stated: "That may seem like a good policy on your part, but you will find that not only will your giving to the Mission and Service fund start to drop, your giving to local projects and the regular budget of the congregation will also diminish. People give to ministry and mission within a church, not to buildings or furnaces." One brave soul on the patriarchal committee, a representative from the United Church Women, spoke up: "It already has happened—I have helped with counting the offering the last three weeks and I have noticed our giving is sliding for local programs and the Mission and Service Fund."

The committee was clearly dumbfounded by both my remarks and the information from one of their members. They were skeptical about the advice I had given, and I am unable to say that my words changed their pattern of seeking support. But something happened because the congregation re-invented their vision of living the gospel with hope.

The aforementioned gift of $50,000 was given eighteen years after that initial discussion, and it was a reminder that some people did not accept the philosophy that we should "pay ourselves" first, but rather that we should think of others. (Some people in the United Church think the donor of that money was that same United Church Women member who never forgot the commitment she carried to God's wider mission.) If we are to be reinventing our vision for living the gospel with hope, where would such a vision come from?

Hearing the Voice of Jesus and Responding

One of the most insightful biblical references to the power of hearing the voice of Jesus and being called to respond is found in the Gospel of John. We read there the story about the call of the first disciples, Andrew and Simon, and are informed that as John the Baptist sees Jesus walk by, he identifies Jesus as the "Lamb of God." These two former disciples of John immediately follow Jesus, and so Jesus turns and asks them: "What are you looking for?" They answer by asking, "Where are you staying?" A classic congregation discussion, is it not? So often when asked a question, we respond with a question. It is much easier than seeking an answer, or looking for a new direction, or finding a way ahead.

Most of us have experienced that "out" in our lives. Many a teenager has arrived after a pre-set curfew time to answer the worried question of a parent: "Where have you been?" with their own question: "Why do you need to know?" or "Don't you trust me?" or maybe "What's the big deal?" Avoid answering to a sticky situation by changing the discussion through asking a question of your own.

There is some comfort in knowing that the very first disciples answered a question from Jesus with a question. "What are you looking for?" could be the quintessential question to be asked of any seeker of the gospel. If we ponder that question, we come into direct interaction with all that the gospel can and should mean to a believer. It is simultaneously reassuring and challenging.

Yet sometimes it is so overwhelming a question to handle in our lives that we cannot face it. How can we answer a question like, "What are you looking for?" when you are in a loveless marriage, or face an abusive partner, or struggle to support yourself or your family on a minimum wage and see no way out? It is too painful to admit we need help, and life is full of despair and confusion, so we answer the question with our own question: "Who wants to know?" or "Why don't you mind your own business?"

Congregations also make the same terminal mistake. There are critical times when a congregation faces questions about its future, or has an opportunity to re-define its mission within a changing community, and the refusal to deal with those important questions may be the early death knell of the congregation itself.

Have you been there when someone has asked the difficult yet perceptive questions of your congregation? Maybe it was during a board meeting, or as part of a visioning exercise. Maybe the questions were provided by an outside facilitator, or expressed by a relative newcomer to your community. The list of questions and the people who may have asked them can be almost endless, but some common questions are:

1. What are the needs of our neighborhood?
2. How has our community changed in the last twenty-five years? Ten years? Five years? Is our congregation seeking to meet the needs that arise from those changes?
3. What do people seek from the church?
4. How can we enter into partnership with other agencies and community outreach ministries?
5. Does our worship bring life to those who attend and how can it be improved?

When Energy For the Gospel is Renewed, Congregation Giving Increases

Another congregation debated the size of their annual budget, though clearly the wealth of the congregation was such that the budget was well within reach. Once again, as we both have seen far too often in working with congregations in their planning processes, some congregation members felt the best way to reach the spending targets for the year was to reduce the mission giving by 15%. Knowing this was a suicidal procedure, yet also sensing that directly challenging this approach would not work, Bill planned an indirect strike. Several attendees within the congregation were refugees from the former Soviet Republic of Georgia, and they were trying to get friends that were stuck in Turkey to a place of refuge. These individuals attended worship regularly, and had proven themselves to be faithful, caring members of the congregation. They were people who lived their faith daily. They knew the power of prayer, and yet political action in this case also was important.

There was no committee to handle refugee requests in the congregation. The outreach committee already felt stretched with a variety of activities within the downtown community. To Bill, it seemed clear there was only one thing to do. Without warning, one Sunday Bill started his sermon with these words: "Every week, we seek to hear what words the lectionary readings for the day offer us within our lives. That was my intent again today, to share a message that would offer insight and hope as we seek to live the gospel message of Jesus Christ. But God had a different plan. This week I had a visitor to my office who offered a compelling story of friends trapped in another country, unable either to return to their homeland or to get to a safe place to live without fear. They need the help of others. It is a story we need to hear, because I truly believe there are people here who can help, and so I invite Christina forward to share her story."

The congregation was spellbound by the story, and before the day was out individuals had stepped forward to form an ad hoc refugee committee. People offered furniture for these friends even before they arrived—the manse became a storage place in anticipation of the new guests. So much furniture of high quality was received that several apartments of people already in Toronto, living in squalid conditions, were furnished. Over $20,000 was raised that first year, in addition to the furniture, food, and clothing purchased or donated, and even more was raised the second year for the new refugee program. And the regular budget challenge? It was forgotten, for the congregation also increased giving to the local ministry and the denominational Mission and Service Fund. It seems that one act of defiant bravery in worship, allowing a spell-binding story of suffering, challenge, and intrigue to be shared, increased the congregational giving by about $45,000 in one calendar year. Why? People saw the church being the church, and wanted to get on board. They re-invented their vision of living the gospel with hope.

Why People Give

People eagerly give to ministry and mission, the essential way to live the gospel with hope, not to budgets. So how do you conduct a capital campaign and re-furbish or re-energize your physical surroundings based on this principle? One simple approach: see the building as the vehicle through which you live God's mission in the world. Just as the church is the vehicle through which the gospel is shared today, and so is appropriately known as the "Body of Christ," likewise the church building and capital resources that are part of your ministry site form the physical envelope in which ministry and mission happens. So we are not raising money for a building; we are raising money to allow us to meet our goals to share in God's mission effectively and lovingly. It is true we need a building for many activities, but it is to be a building to enable ministry and mission to happen, not a monument to the past or an icon for the future.

Transformational leaders know what is important, and know how to share the gospel in ways that allow everyone to become a part of what is taking place. Transformational leaders know that living the gospel with hope is where our focus must be at all time, and they will keep that focus clear. They do not get sidetracked by the needs of a building nor are they tripped up by the costs related to a building

People are less and less enthusiastic about supporting a church building for its own sake. After all, more and more people within our communities are challenged to have a house of their own, or to meet the monthly payments on their condo or apartment or townhouse. Paying for a building as a symbol to the community is a non-starter, but helping to support a structure that allows for effective ministry to take place, that is a whole different matter. That can excite and motivate a congregation (and indeed a whole community) as they seek to have a space that is welcoming, well-furnished, suitably decorated, and enchanting in appearance in order to welcome people to be a part of the activities housed therein.

We Have the Vision: How We Get People Involved

Jesus not only took a rich person to lunch; he invited himself over to the rich person's home, saying, "Zacchaeus, today I must eat at your house." The meal ended with Zacchaeus pledging to give half of his money to God's work, and agreeing to pay back four times the amount to anyone he had ever cheated.[3]

Transformational leaders give every person the opportunity to live their own spiritual journey and offer them hope by sharing with them the opportunity to share their assets for the benefit of the wider world.

An artist told his friends that he wanted to create a sculpture of God. The friends of the artist said, "You can't sculpt God!" The artist worked diligently for many months and when he had completed his task, his friends came to see the sculpture. When he unveiled the statue, the face changed to different races of humankind according to the angle of the light that shone on the marble, and the arms were cut off at the wrists. The artist's friends asked, "Why doesn't the statue have any hands?" The sculptor replied, "God doesn't have any hands but ours."

Giving is a way of being God's hands. Giving is a way of re-inventing a vision of living the gospel with hope.

Notice Opportunities to Give

Bill and Ed agree that we want to give everyone ample opportunities to give, and to look for such opportunities and create worthy opportunities. Many pastors have a service at an important time of the year (Epiphany, Ash Wednesday, Maundy Thursday, Good Friday, Thanksgiving, Christmas Eve or Christmas morning) where they always take up an offering. I have other colleagues who say that Good Friday or Christmas Eve are the worst times of year to take up an offering. They usually say something like: "We have so many guests that evening, and we should treat them with respect and not ask them for money." That makes no sense. People are moved to come to church for they want to hear a message of peace and goodwill. They have come to seek ways that this life of Jesus can make sense for their

3 James 1:9, Ecclesiastes 3:7.

own lives. They seek to face important issues within their own lives. They are moved to look beyond themselves, and if we do not offer a way for them to express their thanks and their desire to help others, we stifle their spiritual journey. Thanks to us, we have taken away a key part of someone's Christmas or Easter spiritual journey when we refuse a chance to allow people to give to the needs of others out of their own heartfelt generosity. How much more can we do to destroy the effectiveness of the gospel in our time than to deny people's need for being generous, caring people? Once one experiences the generosity of God, one wants to be generous in return. No, one *needs to be* generous in return. We want to be invitational in the ways that we seek such involvement and commitment, but we do not deny people a chance to make a difference. The gospel is not all about me. Our sermons remind us of that; our scripture readings remind us of that; our offering reminds us of that. Enough said.

When Giving is Seen as Excessive

Most families can tell stories of "what it was like in the old days" and those stories often include tough times. In our family, my father was not a good money manager. In fact, there were many times that he would simply give what he had to someone in need. He reasoned that he would have another paycheck coming in. My mother tells the story little differently. She tells of times when our family did not have enough money to buy groceries, because my father had given our money to people in need. This is an example of how even the gift of giving can become a curse when it is practiced in excess. Of course, "excess" is a matter of interpretation.

Bill remembers travelling through the hill country of Kentucky in the middle of the afternoon as his family returned from a spring trip to Florida. It was probably the biggest vacation he enjoyed as a child, and that day his father announced they would not pack a lunch but would eat at a restaurant. The excitement of this opportunity waned as they traveled further into the Appalachians without finding a restaurant. At about 1:30 p.m. they stopped at a roadside rest area, and his father fed the last crackers and piece of bread in their picnic basket to a mangy dog scrounging for food. Now they had nothing to east, and no eatery in sight. In the end, they did eat within an hour, and the experience became a symbol of trusting that sustenance would be provided, but for a young boy the fear of being hungry dominated the experience. Too often we see generosity as excessive when we let fear about the future control us. Why are we so hesitant to trust God?

Barb is very generous. She has the spiritual gift of giving. She notices opportunities to give and enjoys being generous. One day at the meal table, she said, "As you know, I went to Catholic parochial school every year, and I would like to give $500 to my Catholic school." Her non-Catholic husband was nonplussed, "You've got to be kidding!" And yet he says that from that day on he realized that, while giving also can be seen to be in excess, "When Barb suggests something she wants to give, I would be wise to hear the voice of God supporting her spiritual gift."

Of course we give to our children, grandchildren, partners, parents and friends. Those are examples of giving within our walls, and they are certainly good giving habits. These are universal examples of giving. Giving to our congregation is also an example of giving within our family of faith.

It is a simple shift to turn from giving "to" our congregation to giving "through" our congregation to those who don't have family to support them or enough food or adequate shelter. It is fulfilling to give to those in need. It is fulfilling because it is living the gospel message. Bill's mother when she was able (before several years in a nursing home) gave over 20% of her retirement income to the church, for her living needs were minimal. Bill says: "My mother was spending my inheritance in supporting The United Church of Canada, so I thought it made sense that I work for the denomination in the area of stewardship." Most of us in our congregations would be better off if we heeded the wise counsel of a popular auctioneer in rural Ontario a generation ago. He often was heard to say as two people were engaged in heated bidding, driving the price of an article beyond what most would deem to be its actual worth, "Don't worry at all. I will tell you when you have bid too much." God will tell us when we have been too generous. Most of us are in no danger of reaching that level.

We sometimes quote the verse, "God shows no partiality."[4] But Jesus was partial to those who are oppressed, and to those who are handcuffed

4 Acts 10:34.

by poverty, sickness, prison, hunger, and thirst. When we give to those beyond our walls, Jesus tells us that we are doing it for him.[5]

Moving From 'What' to 'Why'

Our motive for giving is not to take credit, or contrast it with others who don't give, or to earn a tax deduction. Our motive is a joyful one, and it is a joy that comes from gratitude, simply giving as Jesus gave, even dying for us.

By all means "check out" the legitimacy of a charitable organization. Verify what percentage of your gift will actually go to the expressed need. On the other hand, postponing all giving until after we have checked out each recipient can be excessive. Spontaneous giving to someone with a cardboard sign that says "out of work" could of course result in the recipient spending your small gift in a way you might not approve of, but that is not your concern. One author says that is beyond our "circle of control."[6]

Get in the habit of giving as often as opportunities arise. Those opportunities are God's gift to us. We may not even realize that we have given something to another in the name of Jesus.

Bill recently returned to Toronto to live, and so most Saturday mornings he goes to the St. Lawrence market, a popular downtown market with an assortment of vendors, looking for meat, eggs, bread, and vegetables. Outside the north market early in the morning stands Kenny who sells weekly newspapers in hopes of making a few dollars. Bill has known Kenny for close to twenty years, but he says something changed the day he stopped looking at Kenny as a homeless person who used drugs, possibly drank too much, and clearly ate poorly, to seeing him as a child of God who needed to be shown the common care and decency deserving of any child of God. Suddenly Kenny was not a statistic, or a misfit, or a forlorn forgotten person, but someone for whom God cared deeply, and so must I. It took some time for that attitude to be completely transformed, but now Bill seeks out Kenny at his selling stall, and Kenny engages in conversation with his head up, usually making eye contact, because he is treated as an equal in life by at

5 Matthew 25:34–45.
6 Stephen Covey.

least one person. Living the Gospel with hope means sharing that hope with those who most need it. And new insight bursts forth when we recognize that those who most need it also are those who most deserve it in God's eyes.

Giving Our Time

A middle-class couple we know learned about a need for hearing aids in Russia and Belarus, where eight thousand identified individuals were not able to hear their loved ones or what was going on in worship. That turned into a life-changing experience, not only for the people they served, but also for the couple. They list that giving opportunity as one of their most memorable life experiences.

The story is told of a man who saw another shivering in the cold, and he took off his coat and put it around the shoulders of the shivering one, and went on his way. When Jesus welcomed the man into heaven, the man was surprised and asked, "Why should I get into heaven? I haven't done anything worthy, and I certainly haven't done anything for you." Jesus replied, "There is nothing you could have done that would make you worthy of everlasting life. However, you have done much for me. Do you remember when you put your coat over the shoulders of that shivering man? I was that shivering man."

Never be Afraid to Invite People to Give: It's an Opportunity

The fear of asking for gifts on Christmas Eve often spills over into our approach for funding the ministry of the congregation throughout the year. We should never be afraid to ask people to share in God's mission. If we believe in what we do and who we are as a congregation, then our passion and commitment should be contagious.

Have you ever been near an NFL stadium the morning of a big game? Seen the excitement of the tailgate parties? Gazed upon the fans in their team colors and painted faces? None of them comes up to a passerby and says: "I would like to invite you to share in the excitement of this moment but I realize you may not have the resources to party with us, or you may not fully understand all of the symbolism of this exercise on a Sunday morning, or you may not know much about football or where our team is in the current standings, so I will not embarrass you by inviting you into our gathering." No, it is a celebration, and all are welcome to share in the excitement. Anything you need to know about football or the local team you learn through engaging the enthusiastic crowd in the parking lot. Should not the church be at least as welcoming on a Sunday morning, and indeed on every day of the year? Do you ever think of having a Sunday morning tailgate party in your congregation to celebrate the opportunity to live the gospel with hope?

Receiving Opportunities to Give Our Gifts in Themselves

Once people are part of our community they want to be a part of all aspects of the community. Setting standards of giving to a new member may be somewhat daunting, but an invitation that simply states, "We welcome your presence and involvement, including ways to share your gifts" need not be intimidating.

One year the stewardship focus at a congregation in which Bill was the minister seemed to sputter to the starting gate. Only three people, including him, agreed to serve on the committee.

A low-key approach was decided, but Bill insisted that each person would receive a personally signed letter, not a printed letter with a stamped signature. The other two members of the committee picked names of people they knew and felt comfortable approaching, since their name would be the signature on the letter of invitation. Bill himself chose to write to people no one else knew and to a select group of people he felt needed a special invitation.

One such person he knew well through conducting the funeral of this individual's partner a year earlier. This man attended church almost every Sunday with his adult daughter. They sat in the same place, listened intently to the weekly message, quietly participated in worship. They never came to church dinners or fundraising events or special concerts or mid-week services. But they were there each week—Sunday after Sunday. Clearly the regular worship time was very important to them, and Bill wanted to acknowledge that in his letter to them.

So he did not just sign the letter (most letters in his pile received a note of some kind), but wrote a carefully crafted, heart-filled note: "Thank you for your presence and your interest in worship each Sunday. We are blessed by your commitment to be regularly in our midst. Sincerely, Bill."

He made no rousing requests for giving to the congregation and to God's mission beyond the letter itself. No pulling at the heartstrings of a still grieving widower to demand more from him than was appropriate. No making the individual feel guilty for living a simple faith commitment Sunday by Sunday where others gave of themselves in numerous hours within other activities and projects. All he did was offer a simple and direct "thank you" for the clear, deep commitment the man and his daughter lived out through worship each and every week.

The letters went out on a Wednesday, and in a small city probably were received by Friday. Monday morning the recipient of this letter arrived at the church office. Bill could hear him speaking to the church administrator. He recognized the voice so went out of his office to say hello. In his humble way, this individual said: "I got your letter, Reverend, so I thought I should do what I could. Sorry it was not more."

Bill replied, "Thank you so much; I know you are always caring in what you do and how you give. It is very much appreciated." The man was a retired elementary school janitor, and his now deceased wife had worked in a retail store. They were hard working, frugal people who clearly did not have huge assets. Yet his commitment and generosity were obvious, so Bill was prepared to be overwhelmed by this over-and-above gift.

Notice that the letter spoke about a commitment for the next year, and my note underlined our appreciation for his commitment and attendance week by week. No expectation was laid out for some immediate response of generosity, yet clearly someone does not take the long bus ride downtown (he did not have a car) unless one wants to do something significant.

That was why Bill guessed the check could be $200, maybe even $250, for he sensed whatever the amount it would be a generous way to show how important the church was to this person. Remember, this gift was over and above his weekly commitment.

Bill was floored when the administrator shared that this individual had donated $1,500 to the congregation's ministry.

Inviting Directly

Inviting directly can also spur surprising generosity. Remember the story of the refugee appealing for help to get her friends into Canada from Turkey? The first person to arrive at the church to support the ad hoc refugee fund created that day was a retired social worker who had spent her career working with people in downtown Toronto. Many of the clients she saw were products of situations where they were abused, living on the street, or malnourished due to poverty challenges. Some had been refugees themselves, struggling to be accepted in their new land. In many ways, her presence that morning did not surprise me, for she was one of the most passionate and caring members of the outreach committee. She no longer could be as active as she once was, but volunteered to call members to remind them of the monthly meetings. She always had a story to share, and always asked about the family of the person she was calling. Her genuine concern for others meant I was not surprised when she came to give a gift for the refugee work.

Yet despite that background, I was not prepared for her story. "I want to help these refugees, because I know how frightening it can be to be alone and have no place to call home. I was once homeless in my early twenties, and I promised God at that time that if I am ever in a situation where I can help someone else who is homeless, I would do so. I am sorry I cannot do more."

Once again, I assumed the generosity would be measured in hundreds of dollars, as her small pension from social work was now over twenty years old. Inflation had to be eating into her resources, making her retirement life far from ostentatious.

When she left, another miracle had been experienced. She had given a check for $1,500 to the refugee fund. Now that particular church had people who could write a $1,500 check about as easily as you or I could give $50 or $100. This woman was not in that category. Of greater significance, as far as I know, no one else wrote a check of that magnitude. She gave because she had lived the story of these refugees, she knew their pain and loneliness, and she wanted to share the love of Christ with them.

Just Let People Know What We're About

We can help people identify with who we are and what we do as a congregation when we make concrete the nature of what we are about.

One year Bill helped a congregation renew its sense of mission with the downtown by inviting very specific gifts to a downtown mission. The church had a commitment to help fund the Salvation Army shelter annually, and had a budget of $8,000 to do just that. The previous two years, donations had dwindled, to the point where during the previous calendar year the donations had been less than $6,500. Costs for feeding and housing people in this shelter were modest, so he decided to invite people to give in a unique way.

The first Sunday of Lent he offered the following invitation: "This year throughout Lent we are focusing on the partnership we have with the downtown mission of the Salvation Army. We support their ministry through our monthly donations to local outreach, and I have supported that work with a regular monthly donation of $50. This year I invite you to join me in making a special donation. I have decided to give an extra $25 that will provide shelter and dinner for one person for two nights, or two people for one night. You may not be able to do that, but I invite you to consider a special gift of $10 for two dinners, or even $5 for one dinner, or $3.50 for a lunch. Your gifts will help someone in our community during a lonely time of year."

Pastors need to be able to speak about financial commitment in specific ways, even personal ways. It will inspire no one if you use language such as "I hope you will do your part," or "We need you to respond to this need." It is far more effective when a pastor can speak with clarity of conviction: "This is so important that I am prepared to support this cause (or this ministry, this mission opportunity, or even this congregation) by giving $______, and I invite you to also offer your support." Then what we give is not a burden; it is part of an invitation to join a team.

The invitation included some education. For those who said the annual goal was far too large, Bill subtly pointed out that he gave $50 per month, or $600 per year. His gifts totaled almost 10% of the gifts from the whole congregation the previous year. If only fifteen people gave at that level (and far more than fifteen in a congregation of over three hundred members were capable of giving to that extent), they would reach an annual amount of $9,000—almost a 50% increase from the previous year. The annual goal was not too high.

At the same time, Bill wanted everyone to feel this was an invitation they could respond to. Many members of the congregation lived in the neighborhood in which the church was located, and were in "rent-geared-to-income" apartments. Some people had incomes of less than $500 per month, so even with some relief in their monthly rent they had less than $40 a week in discretionary income. They could never give an extra $25 on the spot, but maybe they could consider a one-time gift of $3.50 for someone's lunch or $5.00 for someone's dinner.

The response was far more wonderful, and more disturbing, than Bill ever could have imagined. The congregation's bookkeeper attended another United Church, but she knew the congregation well, especially the people who lived in the church's neighborhood. Many of them dropped by the office to visit and would personally hand in their donation if they were away. They were known as special individuals, not by envelope number, and their personal financial situation was certainly known by our office person. Some had gone to her with questions around income tax or paper work needed to claim their rent subsidies.

She burst into Bill's office later on the Monday morning after she had dealt with the offering for the day before, the day on which this unique invitation had been shared, and in an elevated voice asked: "What's going on around here?" Bill blinked and had no idea what spurred this first (and, in five years, only) outburst in his office. "I don't know what you mean" Bill replied, perplexed. "Something's going on around here and I want to get to the bottom of it." Still perplexed, Bill tried to get himself more grounded to be able to offer an answer. "It might help me if you explained what you are talking about."

So she began: "I have been doing the offering from yesterday and I see a lot of people have given $5.00, $7.50, even $12.50 and I know they do not have the income to give away money to that extent. Some of these gifts surpass their monthly donations. I want to know what kind of pressure has been put on these people that they feel they must give these amounts."

The worry and anxiety quickly changed to amusement and thanksgiving. "On Sunday I invited the congregation to think about our outreach to the community through the Salvation Army soup kitchen," Bill began.

The look in her eyes told me that this tale had better be good. The explanation continued, repeating the invitation to respond and the various modest amounts listed that people might want to consider giving.

It turns out that most people who responded were folks who understood what it is like to go hungry for a day, or miss a meal for lack of resources. Unlike our caring bookkeeper thought, we did not need to strong-arm people to give. They had responded to an invitation, clearly made, yet softly delivered. They knew the implications of how important their gift was to the people being served, even though it was modest by the world's standards. They had been hungry themselves, and maybe still face days near the end of the month when their own cupboards are bare, so they knew how vital a hot meal can be to someone with few resources. They wanted to reach out to others by living the gospel with hope.

Neither Encourage Guilt Nor Take Blame For the Guilt Others Feel

Often in the church we refuse to ask because we are afraid people will feel guilty if they cannot respond. Any invitation should have room for all to participate. Those who seem to be least able to respond often are those first among the responders. My only disappointment is that our bookkeeper never did come running down the hall to announce that people of greater means had given $25, $50, or more to this effort. Those who responded really did know how hard it is to have enough food to live week by week, and day by day.

Every year within The United Church of Canada congregations in Newfoundland and Labrador are among the churches with the highest increase in giving year over year. In lean years such as 2008 and 2009, they were the congregations with the lowest downturn in giving.

Around the capital city of St. John's there is a mini-boom due to off-shore oil strikes, but for the most part the province is struggling with underemployment, compounded by the collapse of the fishing industry on the seaboards. Yet people without immense resources understand how significant it is to do whatever one can to support others.

It shows transformational leadership to give generously. It is also a natural way to begin re-inventing a vision of living the gospel with hope. Inviting such generosity may be the very wake-up call your congregation is ready for. And it is God-pleasing.

FOR FURTHER DISCUSSION

1. When you go through down times, does it appeal to you to consider re-inventing a vision of living the gospel with hope? How would you begin?
2. If your congregation were to re-invent a vision of living the gospel with hope, where could the idea come from? How could it be promoted and integrated into all that you do?
3. How could your congregation improve the way it encourages people to grow in giving?
4. What would you like someone to say to you when they invite you to give to a worthy cause? Does your church talk about money, or talk about ministry and mission opportunities?
5. Describe a time you gave a generous, even sacrificial gift. How did you feel about it? Why do you suppose you felt that way? Was the gift appropriately honored?

7

Transformation Through Simplifying Our Lives

"Get yourselves a bank that can't go bankrupt, a bank far from bank robbers, safe from embezzlers, a bank you can bank on. It's obvious, isn't it? Where you place your treasure is the place where you will most want to be, and will end up being."[1]

"The farm of a certain rich man produced a terrific crop. He talked to himself, 'What can I do? My barn is not big enough for this harvest.' Then he said, 'Here is what I will do: I will tear down my barns and build bigger ones. Then I will gather all my grain and goods. Then I will congratulate myself on how well I've done. I have it made and can now retire. I can take it easy and have the time of my life.' Just then God showed up and said, "Fool! Tonight you die. And your barn full of goods—who gets it?" That's what happens when you fill your barn with self and not with God."[2]

Simplifying Your Life—A Welcome Suggestion

With all the complexities life brings, for many of us it comes as a welcome suggestion to consider simplifying our lives. We can do so by thinking paradoxically—by seeing the truth in two opposite statements. We realize "on the one hand..." and also "on the other hand..." The human brain has difficulty arranging those two opposites to fit simultaneously. We accept that. Thinking paradoxically simply makes room for two opposites to exist side-by-side.

1 Luke 12:34, Eugene Peterson, *The Message.*
2 Luke 12:13–21, Eugene Peterson, *The Message.*

For example, God's Word says that we can do nothing good on our own[3] and also that we can do all things through Christ.[4] How can this be? Those opposites comprise a paradox. Both are true and accurate. What is amazing is that you and I can simplify our lives by dealing with many conflicting signals we get about life by discerning which opposites form a paradox and then embracing the paradox rather than resisting it. This is a little-known secret in many congregations.

Embracing Paradox

In the movie "Fiddler on the Roof," Tevye struggles with paradox. He converses with God, "Why did you make so many poor people? I know it is no disgrace to be poor; but then it is no great honor, either." He also struggles with the paradox of change and tradition. And he struggles with the paradox of loving his daughters, all five of whom decide differently than their Jewish tradition. One decides to marry a ne'er-do-well businessman. Another simply leaves home. A third falls in love with a Russian soldier. In one poignant sentence, Tevye says," I can't bend any further," and he decides, in that moment, to disown his daughter rather than accept the paradox. But there is an alternative.

Replacing Complicating With "Complexifying"

Complexifying is a word used in narrative therapy to estimate the effect of a dominant issue on our lives. It creates a paradigmatic shift that enables a person to discover a capacity for changing what previously seemed to be intractable.

We use complexifying as an approach in congregation conflict management. We invite the person or group to estimate the impact of an issue on their lives. If it appears that a particular issue affects one's life 85% of the time, that's a very different challenge than if the person says it impacts his or her life 15% of the time.

Sam is an investment counselor. Over the years, we have brought him many questions. Most of the time, however, Sam answered, "It depends."

3 Psalm 14:1, 3; Romans 3:12.
4 Philippians 4:13.

At first we were irritated with that answer, as though he were trying to avoid the question. Yet the more we listened and worked together, the more we understood the narrative principle called complexifying, which simply means exploring the maximum number of areas in which a particular idea affects our lives.

President Harry Truman had no success when he tried to deal with the economic issues of his day without embracing paradox. On one occasion he summoned the finest economists to his office to get him some answers. When he was in conversation with the highly respected leaders, he simply posed one question, "What is the economy going to be like in the next few years?" It sounds simple enough, doesn't it?

One economist replied, "On the one hand, things look very difficult and dark and gloomy; on the other hand, things will stabilize." Another economist replied, "I agree. On the other hand, things might not stabilize and the economy could very well get worse." A third economist said, even more boldly, "Both of the previous economists are correct. On still another hand, the economic situation is so bad that if we don't take immediate action we could have a global meltdown." A fourth economist added, "All of that is accurate. On the other hand, we are headed to one of the best economic times we've ever had."

President Truman was nonplussed. He said, "What this world needs is a one-handed economist." He had difficulty embracing the paradox that the opposites could be accurate at the same time.

Complexification helps us to recognize not only the power of an idea to handcuff but also to perceive "measurable" progress. We consider it a God-given capacity that is available to everyone. It visibly demonstrates the paradox that a skill can be perceived and implemented even before it is consciously learned. In order to illustrate how our lives can identify and embrace paradox, let's identify some faith paradoxes.

Faith Paradoxes

Our faith contains many paradoxes. They can transform our discernment. The early Christians wrestled with paradoxes, and the evidence was formalized in three major creeds—the Apostle's Creed, the Nicene Creed, and the

Athanasian Creed. In each case, scholars deliberated for years before accepting paradoxes rather than capitulating to logic. We list them as questions for your participation:

1. Is Jesus human or divine? Yes.
2. Is God one or three? Yes.
3. Are ministers ordained or are we all ministers? Yes.
4. Is God merciful or just, loving or punishing? Yes.
5. Are we saved by faith alone or is faith without works dead faith? Yes.
6. Are we in bondage to sin every day or are we free from sin? Yes.
7. Is our everlasting life a gift or are we to live righteous lives? Yes.
8. Is it natural for us to be generous or stingy? Yes.
9. Was Jesus fully human or free from sin? Yes.
10. Are we sinners or saints? Yes.

Sometimes God may create a paradox by reframing a previous decision. For example, "I will make a new covenant with you."[5] The new covenant did not make the old covenant obsolete. But it clearly superseded the previous understanding.

Jesus created specific paradoxes simply by re-framing "it is said" into "but I say unto you," thus reinterpreting traditional understanding. For example, "You have heard it said by them of old time, you shall not commit adultery: but I say unto you, whoever looks at a woman to lust after her has already committed adultery with her in his heart."[6] Again, Jesus said, "Obey the commandments,"[7] and "A new commandment I give you."[8]

Jesus Christ frees us from the shackles of prejudice and blind rigidity. The apostle Paul says that we can already claim transformation, for "Christ has set us free to live a free life, so take your stand! Never again let anyone put a harness of slavery on you."[9] Freedom is not the same as license. This too is paradox. Free in Christ—now that's transformation. God's love is stronger than our hate.

5 Jeremiah 31:31.
6 Matthew 5:28.
7 Matthew 28:20, Galatians 5:3.
8 Matthew 22:37–40.
9 Galatians 5:1.

Embracing vs. Resisting

Embracing paradox is wiser than resisting it. Resisting trends in paradoxes often makes those issues worse. What we resist intensifies; and what we embrace mellows. Whether we fully understand something or not may not be relevant. The bigger question remains: "Do we understand the intent of the person in this instance?" When someone says repeatedly, "I don't understand" it can actually be a form of manipulation. We can be adept at looking for head reasons as to why something should be embraced, or resisted, while refusing to appreciate the intent underlying the instruction or invitation.

We have a right to be skeptical of those with authority over us. While authority and power are important assets, it is also true that, as Lord Acton said, "Power corrupts, and absolute power corrupts absolutely." On the one hand, "Money is good;" on the other hand, "the love of money is the root of all evil."[10] The power of anger can control us; so can the power of love.

You have likely heard the verse that describes the universal paradox of all people, "The things I want to do with all my heart I do not do; and the things that I want to avoid with all my heart, those things I do."[11] This is so complex that none of us can completely comprehend it, and it is also so simple that a four-year-old can accept it. It is both impossible and simple.

In short, life is more than knowing what we should do; life is a constant struggle to find the appropriate path for the future, given all that we have faced and all that will unfold in the future. Transformational leaders are prepared to search for a way ahead in the midst of such uncertainty.

There is also the matter of choice in how we look at paradoxes. Two men were talking. One said, "I feel like I have two wolves inside me. How can I know which one is going to show up?" The other answered, "Whichever one you feed." There are many wolves, among them immediate gratification, greed, consumerism, and thinking that our way is the only right way. Do we feed our obsessions, or allow God's spirit to feed us?

10 1 Timothy 6:10.
11 Romans 7:15.

Parables Rock Our Preconceptions

Jesus' parables are sometimes seen as moralistic stories in the traditions of earlier commentators, when they really are stories that rock our traditional understanding of the world. They encourage us to see the world and God in new and surprising ways.

Dominic Crossan captures the impact of Jesus' teaching on the parables: "Jesus spoke of God in paradoxical parables but the tradition spoke of Jesus as the Paradoxical Parable of God." [12] Jesus offers a whole new way of seeing the kingdom of God through multi-layered parables (their polyvalent nature), and also offers us a non-formulaic response to God, and indeed, of understanding how God responds to our needs (the paradoxical nature).

For a congregation that feels lost looking for an answer for its future, there is good news in all of this: THERE IS NO ONE RIGHT ANSWER.

The Fallacy of Depending on Past Provisions

A favorite book of mine illuminates Jesus' teachings through other writers of parables. I consider it important in my devotional and teaching life. The author's parable below [13] can assist those who seek ways to transform the congregation:

> *I gave orders for my horse to be brought round from the stable. The servants did not understand me. I myself went to the stable, saddled my horse and mounted. In the distance I heard a bugle call, I asked, "What does this mean?" The servants said they heard nothing. The security guard at the gate stopped me and asked, "Where are you riding to, master?"*
>
> *"I don't know," I said, "Only away from here, away from here. Always away from here, for only by doing so can I reach my destination."*

---

12 Quote from John Dominic Crossan, Cliffs of Fall: *Paradox and Polyvalence in the Parables of Jesus,* Seabury Press, 1980. This book, though almost 35 years old, has been reprinted

13 One of several examples of modern parables that interact with Jesus' parables, this one from Kafka, found in Robert Funk, *Jesus as Precusor,* Augsburg Fortress Publishing, 1975.

"Do you know your destination?" he asked.

"Yes," I answered, "didn't I say so? Away-From-Here, that is my destination."

"You have no provisions with you," he said.

"I need none," I said, "the journey is so long that I must die of hunger if I don't get anything on the way. No provisions can save me. For it is, fortunately, a truly immense journey."

The author emphasizes that the work of congregation transformation is truly an immense journey, and that often carrying along the provisions that have worked in the past for congregations—liturgy, music, preaching, ornate buildings, formal settings, set times for worship, bulky hymn books, long pastoral prayers, familiar processes and governance—no longer work.

What to Look For Along the Way of Transformation

We do not have all of the answers for this truly immense journey of transformation, but we know that you will need to find partners along the way who will help you in that transformation. We cannot do this journey alone—as ministers, congregation leaders, individual congregations, or communities of faith. We need to seek partners, and when we embark on the journey we are not always sure where those partners will come from.

Look for opportunities to try new things. We are not implying that we start a new mid-week service with three people committed to attend and a CD player to provide contemporary music. Congregations can show their interest in new ways of conducting worship and engaging people by providing the resources to do just that.

In the last five years many congregations have added audio-visual equipment in the sanctuary to allow for projection of the hymns on screens at the front. Such technology allows people to set aside the heavy hymn books and sing joyfully, with their heads held high, glorifying and praising God in the midst of the community. The technology also allows for appropriate images to be associated with the prayers of the day and the scriptural passages being read. The sermon can be interspersed with YouTube videos or a particularly insightful blog message.

Congregations often spend a significant amount of money to install equipment and then they fail to equip people to use the new resource in a helpful way. Change for the sake of change is not helpful. The potential is great. Look for new ways to share the message and engage people in worship. It will take change. It will take money. It will take commitment. It will take perseverance. It will take faith. Are you up to it?

Make No Small Plans

"Make no small plans, for there is no magic in them to stir your soul."[14] Anything God gives us the capacity to conceive, we can achieve with God's help. God gives us the capacity to dream, and God gives us the capacity to make the dream come true.

"If anyone is in Christ, he is a new creature."[15] This is neither illusion nor fantasy. Consider the larva as it morphs into a chrysalis, and then goes through metamorphosis from the chrysalis to a butterfly.

What is significant about this transformation within the cycle of a butterfly is the struggle to emerge from the chrysalis stage into a full-fledged butterfly. It seems painful and unnecessarily challenging as we watch the process unfold. But it is part of the process of transformation for the butterfly. The worst thing someone can do is try to speed up the process. The emerging butterfly gets the strength in its wings to fly by struggling to escape its protective shield. If someone opens the chrysalis prematurely the butterfly will not be able to fly.

If you want to be a leader in congregational transformation, read on. There is no "transformation-in-a-box" kit. Techniques and tools are helpful, but the simple first step in transformation is for the leader to identify a champion who has energy for the idea, any idea. Champions may emerge on their own when they read your "Volunteers Needed" notice, but most of us are not inspired by those two words.

Leaders build teams. The leader identifies a possible champion with energy for the idea. Without a champion, there will be no transformation,

14 David Schwartz, *Make No Small Plans.*
15 2 Corinthians 5:17

but the leadership role is to identify, enlist, and train the potential champion. The newly-emerging butterfly learns to fly. Whatever spiritual gift is needed is available. One way to spot a champion is to invite their stories. Listen to their story and watch where the energy emerges like a beautiful butterfly.

The larva cannot imagine flying in the air instead of crawling in the dirt all its life. So it is with people before someone helps them identify their passions and gifts. But once a butterfly, it has no desire to crawl in the dirt anymore. Put a bigger frame around your picture. Trade in your small box for a bigger box. See how it changes you. Think abundance rather than scarcity. Scarcity thinking can ruin your life.

The children of Israel wallowed in scarcity. They complained. They found the negative. They were in the habit of complaining so much that finally God got tired of their complaining and simply said, "Trip canceled." Avoid negativity as well as the paralysis of analysis. Those two tendencies threaten transformational leadership. If the idea has already become complicated, it is not too late. Simplify it. "Keep it simple" may be the biggest principle.

How to Know When Your Plan is Big Enough

Because they know that God gives abundance, transformational leaders make big plans. One way to accomplish that is with SMART goals (Specific, Measurable, Achievable, Realistic, and Timely). Another way to look at it comes from our HealthierChurch.org Coach, John Gillespie, who says, "Make plans that are so big that only God can accomplish them." Can goals be too big?

Do you want to know if your goal is big enough? Pray, "Holy Spirit, reveal to me any unconfessed sin in my goal." You will get your answer. That is the transformation Jesus offers when he promises, "I am come that they might have life and life in all its abundance."[16]

Jesus simplifies the Torah, reduces the code of the Pharisees and their multitudinous rules. When Jesus was asked, "What is the greatest commandment?" Jesus did not reply, "That depends; there are many

16 John 10:10.

commandments." He answered succinctly, "Love the Lord your God with all your heart, with all your soul, and with all your mind."[17] Then he anticipated the next question, "What is the second greatest commandment?" and answered it by announcing, "Love your neighbor as yourself."[18]

Jesus' intent was not to make things easy, but to enable us to keep it simple. And yet that simplicity can be distorted when we forget, even for a moment, that loving God and others is infinite, just as God's unconditional love and patience is infinite for us.

Avoid Surface Issues: They Are Usually Distractions

Congregations sometimes make mountains out of mole hills, forgetting to keep the main thing the main thing. Our experience has been that the presenting issue is seldom the real issue, but rather only a surface one. The underlying issue is usually something that distracts us from God's mission. When we focus on God's mission in our congregation, many of the so-called "other issues" pale in comparison.

No one principle of transformational leadership stands alone. Pastors are especially adept at integrating principles and practices over time. "Keep it simple, but don't expect it to be easy" is an example of such a principle. It is integrated with other principles as it is applied in day-to-day congregation life. In the Holy Spirit, it is simple—however difficult it may be to live it out.

Part of the Big Plans one makes in ministry is to look for the long term in what one does. There may be wisdom in having a five to eight-year plan when you enter into a new ministry. On the other hand, you may not stay that long in a congregation if your ministry calls you to communities where the pattern of movement transpires more rapidly.

Having a longer plan can be helpful for most of us. Otherwise, if we only look ahead for three years or less, by the time year two rolls around to us, we are already planning an exit strategy, or considering a new focus. Long range planning (for ten, twenty, or more years) is virtually impossible in our shifting society.

---

17 Matthew 22:37.
18 Matthew 22:39.

It may be helpful to look at least four or five years ahead. However, in our current cultural climate, "long term" means six months. We still need a well-designed strategic plan, but we must be flexible in order to make room to modify our initial plans and vision. Of utmost importance is the fact that we must keep our eyes on the mission—e.g., God's mission. Without a longer view, our default is emergency planning or ad hoc management. We are not so much planning, in that case, as we are reacting to what is happening around us. If we see ourselves as working as partners with God, then we must find ways to plan ahead. But as God's partners, we also must be flexible. There are times when God may surprise us, and we need to be ready to respond, helpfully and positively, to those surprises.

Imagine How Your community Was Planned

Look around your neighborhood. If you are fortunate enough, as we are, to live in city regions that have tall, majestic trees offering shade on your block, realize that many of those trees were planted by people who no longer live in your neighborhood, or may not even be alive.

Few trees would be planted in our world if we only planted trees we expected to see grow into maturity within our own lifespan. The same can be said of planting ideas within your congregation. Plan big, plan for the future, plan with a longer view ahead. Jesus says, "Seek first the kingdom of God, and all these things will be added unto you."[19] You are not trying to control your future, but seeking to be a part of God's future in your congregation and community.

When we say, "Don't make any small plans," that doesn't mean that we are to ignore the details. Some plans are too big to understand fully, so they must begin small. You may wonder, if you have read the parables of Jesus, "What do you mean by not making small plans?"

Jesus seemed to talk incessantly about small plans, or at least used small, ordinary realities to portray his understanding of God's realm. He spoke of a mustard seed, the smallest of all seeds, that becomes a plant large enough for birds to nest in its shade. He spoke of a woman sweeping

19 Matthew 6:34.

the floor to find a lost coin. He spoke of a person finding buried treasure in a large field—a pearl, a small reality. I especially like the parable of a shepherd looking for one lost sheep in the wilderness and risking the lives of ninety-nine other sheep to look for that one.

Jesus often tells stories that set us on edge, and that turn our expectations upside down as to who or what God can be:

1. In a religious tradition where cedar and oak trees represented the power of God, Jesus turned to a mustard seed.
2. In a society that honored the religious leaders in their ornate robes, Jesus lifted up the ordinary activity of a housewife sweeping the kitchen floor to speak about God's care and resourcefulness.
3. In a world where the temple was filled with gold and ornaments, Jesus imagined a small pearl as capturing the essence of God's wonder.
4. In a world where doing the right thing and the safe thing was celebrated, Jesus went out looking for those who have strayed from the path and entered into an existence that was close to being self-destructive.

Picture Jesus' upsetting words. The parables often changed the unique traditional roles that we have associated with each of the characters. For example, we knew (or so we thought) the parable of the lost sheep was about the lost sinner, and Jesus, as the shepherd (of the congregation or community) goes out to rescue lost sinners. That's one understanding.

Another understanding surfaces if it is not Jesus or the congregation that is the shepherd. We as individuals might be the shepherds, and the lost sheep might be God, who has become lost in our lives through the desire to maintain our home and two cars and three televisions and four bedrooms and.... Can you see how that shifts the point of the story and transforms the reader into a new awareness of what Jesus may be saying?

If we like the traditional imagery of saving the lost sinner as that which is upheld in the story of the shepherd seeking the lost sheep, then the story of the housewife sweeping her kitchen floor can only be understood by that same approach if we see the housewife as God and the lost coin as a symbol of the lost soul. No wonder Jesus upset people by portraying God in such simple, and unconventional, ways.

We are not suggesting that the characters of the parables are like allegories. Allegories tend to narrowly define the characters in a formulaic way. The characters tend to be contrasted and compared from other stories in life.

We can see much that is new and exciting in the parables if we allow ourselves to read them with new eyes. There is much that is exciting and possible in our local congregations if we are prepared to see God's mission, and our ministry in response to that mission, with new eyes, and if we are prepared to hear the gospel with new ears. And unless we truly see Jesus' teachings as basic transformational theology, we will struggle with God's call to change and transform our history and tradition.

Little Things Also Matter

Little incremental things are important. To close our eyes to the details is to turn big plans into greater fantasies. Perhaps you have heard the riddle, "How do you eat an elephant?" The answer is, "One bite at a time."

We do not impose a human timetable on the plan. More on this later. We sometimes deceive ourselves with mottos and bromides such as, "It takes seven years to change a culture," or, "You have to have a sufficient inventory to supply a year of sales." Think of a time when culture changed in an instant, or when the only inventory you needed was a single sample.

Congregations are notorious for taking a year or more to develop a mission statement, vision statement, or a strategic plan. In truth, congregations actually make some decisions quite rapidly. When a new idea comes along, we sometimes decide to do it immediately. On the other hand, think how long we may delay in deciding when to let go of an idea that has become obsolete.

While process is vital, it is not absolute. How we discuss our differences and come to a consensus need not be protracted. How long it takes for someone to make a point in a discussion is not based on the average length of time an extrovert takes to do so. Council meetings don't have to last more than an hour, or ninety minutes at most, if we simply set that as the standard. Sometimes it's as simple as doing one's homework or projecting how long we need to discuss each agenda item thoroughly.

If someone were to announce on a Sunday morning that a family in your community had a house fire the night before, and they were left without clothes, personal belongings, food, and a place of shelter, how many hours of meetings would precede the community's decision to offer food, shelter, clothing, support? Wouldn't people rally immediately? In our congregations at times we can be so organized in our governance structures that we miss obvious opportunities to serve. Crises and tragedies may motivate us to act. Why not simply be committed to act when we address every day happenings?

Transformational leadership principles are action-oriented. Transformational leaders make progress and focus continually on action items. Sometimes a minuscule action item might be all it takes to get a big plan off the ground, especially with God's help.

Making Commitment a Regular Activity

One of the major errors in congregations is the way we look at new people who come along into our congregations. When financial struggles bubble to the surface, newcomers may be evaluated as to how much money they can (and will) give to the congregation. Such thinking is harmful, and wrong-headed.

What is significant in terms of living one's commitment within the congregation is not one's assets or cash flow, but one's faith commitment. As we nurture the faith journey of our people, we find that they will want to be regularly a part of worship, and regular contributors to the work of the congregation.

What is far more significant in terms of the financial and spiritual well-being of a congregation is a sense of regular commitment and involvement. That is why we suggest people find ways to make their financial giving a regular activity. What is most important is the regularity of the gift, not initially the size of the gift.

People who increase their commitment usually increase their financial and volunteer activity within a congregation. But if they are not in the habit of regular financial support to the congregation, then that increase may taper off into an insignificant amount.

The United Church of Canada runs a Pre-Authorized Remittance (or PAR) program through the General Council office that allows congregations to encourage members to give monthly through automatic bank withdrawal. Once people give in a regular monthly way, they have decided that supporting the congregation's ministry is significant to them. Then as they increase their involvement and interest in the congregation, they can find ways to increase their commitment through time, activity, and monetary gifts.

Bill tells the story that as a twelve year-old he had envelopes, and gave twenty-five cents a week in those envelopes from his $1 a week allowance. He thought he caught up whenever he was away for a Sunday, but it turned out at the end of the year that he had only given his twenty-five cents for fifty of the fifty-two weeks in the year. That amount, $12.50 for the year, put him above 25% of donors at his home congregation. Many had given nothing, but others gave $2, $5, or even $10 for the year, probably gifts that represented an infrequent attendance pattern. A modest but regular offering from a young person made a difference to the financial well-being of the congregation. When we encourage our members to give regularly rather than focusing on the size of the gift, we establish opportunities for participation that includes us all.

Simplifying congregation life is more enjoyable, less anxiety-producing, and more transformational. And it is God-pleasing.

FOR FURTHER DISCUSSION

1. What would it look like if you simplified your life? What parable can you think of that might help you do so?
2. Make a list of attributes of Jesus. Which attributes are paradoxes? Is God merciful and just? How can we embrace both?
3. Take some time to discuss how embracing paradox can greatly simplify your life.
4. Do you feel more comfortable by making small plans for activity within your congregation or more inspired by making big plans? Why do you suppose that is?
5. Describe something you learned in this chapter, and how it appeals to you as you travel along the journey of transformation. How does God's presence with you make it even more appealing?

8

Transformation Means Take Your Time Quickly

"We were not idle when we were with you, and we did not eat anyone's bread without paying for it; but with toil and labor we worked night and day, so that we might not burden any of you."[1]

As we look around at others we can easily see that, on the one hand, there is too much rushing. Everybody's in a hurry. We all have experiences when we would just like to slow things down a bit. On the other hand, we can also see that there is an epidemic of taking more time than necessary. So here's the paradox: We suggest that you take your time quickly.

Transformational leadership in "taking our time quickly" is not about rushing and it is not about delay. It is about radically decreasing the unnecessary amount of time it takes in our day compared to what it took in the past. The shift is as dramatic as going from horse and buggy to the automobile.

For example, transformational "taking our time quickly" is not about reducing an eight-hour job *by* eight minutes. That is not particularly transformational. Taking our time quickly is about discerning how an eight-hour job can be accomplished *in* eight minutes. Now that's transformational. Taking our time quickly refers to changing how decisions that usually take three months can be accomplished in three hours. That's transformational.

1 2 Thessalonians 3:7b-8.

Before we go any further, however, let's face up to the fact that we will not be able to revitalize our congregations without dismantling the dysfunctional system of governance called committees. Transformational leaders can provide a major service by helping us notice how congregations make decisions.

Rethinking Whether or Not We Need Committees and Boards

Have you ever thought about whether or not we need committees? Certainly, we need organization, accountability, record keeping, accessible information, and a way to manage conflict. But many of those tasks can now be done electronically. Like tweets that limit us to messages of no more than 140 characters, digital communications certainly have their benefits. What do you think would happen in council, session, vestry, or any other leadership team meeting if everyone disciplined themselves to say their piece in 140 characters? Unthinkable? Congregation meetings in which opinions would be texted? Ridiculous? What if speeches were limited to twenty words, and were then opened for discussion, with those comments being limited to twenty words? Are you smiling?

So if committees and boards don't make significant progress in a reasonable time, consider abandoning them. There are alternatives.

Permission-giving, transformational leadership

Let us speak to how we can "take our time quickly" in a major event where we assume arrangements will determine that a lot of time needs to be taken to carry out the plan.

We are associated with HealthierChurch.org. Part of its work is to conduct webinars for congregation leaders year-round. The webinars can be held whenever an individual or group is available. Interaction occurs in real time, either by voice or by text. Many congregations and denominations are using this process for continuing education for pastors and congregation leaders. A succinct, pithy presentation can be viewed in the comfort of your office, or even living room. In less than an hour (travel time included!) new skills may be learned, and new processes understood.

HealthierChurch.org also conducts an annual conference that is available throughout North America. No formal breaks are scheduled. Formal question-and-answer periods are eliminated. Attendance has increased 400% thanks to remote webcasting. The results to date have been amazing. Interaction and discussion has increased by an estimated 1000%. Discussions stay on topic. Introverts appreciate the interaction. Extroverts invest more time thinking about what they're going to say before they say it instead of thinking things out as they are speaking. The presentations and discussions are sent to all participants in real time for those who want them. How special to attend and participate in an international conference in the comfort of one's own home or congregation building, thanks to being connected electronically.

Some congregation leaders cannot imagine "how we can operate without a committee!" Not everyone appreciates discovering that a digital exchange on one question can happen in a few minutes and can at times replace the need for a meeting. Some committees function quite well, but there are alternatives that are being used successfully in many congregations, such as "mission-shaped teams."

From committees to mission-shaped teams

Mission-shaped teams have several characteristics. Team members are focused on mission, and are selected for their passion and spiritual gifts for ministry. These teams get things done more quickly, solve difficulties more easily, and build relationships better. After all, the focus is on growth not on who is the leader or the predetermined tasks. Mission-shaped teams have specific roles they choose, rather than being assigned to them, with a clear starting date and ending date. The leadership team simply supports and encourages them, often asking, "Do you need anything?" and regularly thanking them for their good work. This enables significant progress to occur in a reasonable time, helps relationships develop, and builds morale.

There is Someone Out There Waiting to be Invited

We hear some leaders complain, "Nobody wants to do anything," and sometimes we slip into that habit ourselves. Not only does that destroy rapport with others, it's probably not even accurate. Just the opposite is actually the case. Believe it. Your congregation is filled with people eager to get involved in something significant. People usually welcome the opportunity to participate in a working group, or a mission activity, or an outreach event, or staff a hospitality table, or help out at a community dinner. People hesitate to be on a committee where there are meetings, little chance to make an impact, and a long-term commitment.

When you invite people to share their skills in doing something meaningful, great things can and will happen. The simple reason for the energy is that people want to be involved in significant ways. As evidence, Bill says that when he has offered a volunteer opportunity to a congregation member that significantly matches their interest and spiritual gifts, is time limited, and does not involve being on a committee, he has never been turned down.

Being this kind of transformational leader means identifying action items that can be implemented to enable significant results to occur in a reasonable time. Instead of the motivation being utilitarian, and the end not justifying the means, the transformational leader identifies a journey that is equal in importance to the destination. This way, no one's time feels wasted.

When your life and mine are lived with integrity, it is a powerful force by which to reconcile the world to God in Jesus Christ[2] and all of us to each other. It all happens through the power of the Holy Spirit. It is always offered, and never forced.

Though life is sought without success by emperors, pursued without hope by investors, abused in excess by hedonists, reasoned eruditely by philosophers, it escapes all but the humble. This life in all its abundance is only available by grace, the undeserved and unconditional grace of God, only learned by one primary source textbook, and appropriated only by faith that celebrates surrender. That is the ultimate paradox.

---

2 2 Corinthians 5:19–20.

This "abundant" life, as Jesus calls it, is tested and practiced in the faith community called "congregation." Congregations can become more effective than many other groups, and have demonstrated this for two thousand years. Congregations banded together to establish quality education from the home to the university. Congregations have found effective ways to manage conflict and have championed quality respect for all, especially the oppressed, those in need, and most of all, children.

With others like them, congregations have established quality adoption and social service agencies, quality world relief, quality community improvement, quality disaster response, and quality care for widows and orphans. Congregations have pioneered the abundant life in Christ.

What is especially noticeable in our day is that we take much more time than is needed to establish quality transformation in our community and world. We need to take time quickly.

One of the God-given gifts to people on planet earth is the gift of technology. We do not worship at the altar of technology, but we are awed by people who are created in the image of God as they discover new processes in healthcare and space travel. We hear of teenagers who have made pace-setting inventions. They understand the principle of taking your time quickly. Many of the things that need correction in our world are increasingly urgent. God enables people to develop new life-giving surgeries. God gives us the capacity to make new life-enriching discoveries in the ocean's depths. And God also gives us the tools to have unsurpassed access to knowledge and communication with each other. We can use this knowledge and communication to help reconcile the world to God in Jesus Christ. This challenge is no less urgent. And congregations are uniquely equipped to address these challenges.

One of the greatest threats to transformational leadership is a matter of delay especially when it comes about in giving too much attention to distractions on subjects that are less important. Did you know that one of the main issues and congregations that cause people to complain is worship style?

Centuries ago, worship services began to use marvelous trumpets and flutes and pipe organs and other instruments. Today we use laptops and smart phone to take pictures and videos and have interactive communication with remote webcast sites that enable us see others through slides and film clips and real time sharing, all of which can touch our hearts and draw us closer to Christ. These are gifts from God in giving us the ability to develop inventions that may someday be as important as heating in winter and cooling in summer.

When prayer movements can be broadcast instantly throughout the world for the good of all, and a hundred versions of the Bible are available at no charge on a smart phone, those are gifts from God to be used for the benefit of all. So too are Facebook and Twitter.

When meetings can be held digitally without travel expense, traffic, or risk of travel, and we can get online education and webinars, these too are gifts from God to be used for the common good. So too are cell phones and texting.

There is no need for delay when we can retrieve instant information by looking it up on the Internet. This too is a gift of God-given human ingenuity and we have a deep desire to find and develop a relationship with others. Leonard Sweet does not shy away from the opportunity such technology offers us. He observes that tweets or blogs are "fast, furious, and infectious." [3] Technological innovation can help people connect people. Using such tools will help a church share a message of hope to the world.

We can make a difference in the world beyond what we ever imagined and we have a great capacity to avoid unnecessary delay. No, technology is not the answer to every question. We have yet to establish boundaries for human decency that is urgently needed. We must not delay. Take your time quickly and trust in God.

Though we say it with tongue in cheek, we have many examples that Jesus, without the benefit of technology, did things immediately, especially when people needed help.[4] We still have a lot to learn about how to make significant progress in a reasonable time, while at the same time catching up in developing human relationships.

---

3 Leonard Sweet, *Viral: How Social Networking is Poised to Ignite Revival* (Colorado: WaterBrook Press, 2012), p. 187.

4 Matthew 21:17–19.

A five-year-old child visited his ninety-year-old great-grandmother and said, "Great-grandma, you need to get on the Internet." She responded, "You think I should get on the Internet? For heaven's sake, why do you think I should get on the Internet?" Her great-grandchild said, "The Internet is fantastic. You can find out anything you want to know on the Internet, without waiting." She replied, "That sounds wonderful. How does it do that?" "I just connect to the Internet on my computer, and you can ask me any question you want, and the computer finds the answer on the Internet right away. Do you have a question that you'd like me to get the answer for you on the Internet?" She said, "Well, yes, as a matter of fact, there is. I'd like to know how Aunt Helen is doing."

At Bill's former congregation a member there (who is 105 years old) operates her own computer and is very savvy using her iPhone. She is much more current in terms of modern technology than many people half her age. We are never too old to engage in the benefits of new technologies.

Some of us look to the past and lament; some of us look to the future and despair. We all have the opportunity to look at the tools and opportunities of the present time, and utilize what is available to us in order to make a difference in the world. That opportunity has not changed for our congregations. It was true for Jesus in his time; it is true for us in our time.

We have many opportunities to learn and grow in experience. And we have what may be the greatest avenue in the last 2000 years, namely, the congregation. Together we can do so much more than we can alone. There is so much we can do. Take your time quickly. Don't dally and don't rush. Take your time, *and* don't take any more time than necessary.

Practice thinking quickly. Try making decisions more promptly. Finish the job instead of postponing it. Lose the trivial things at congregation meetings and leadership team meetings. Allow small mission-shaped teams to develop relationships and give them the freedom to begin new ministries for expanding God's mission. People who have that freedom feel trusted. Transformational congregations create mission-shaped teams, give them the mission statement, and support the mission-shaped team decisions for taking action and implementing new ministry as often as possible.

This is a big opportunity for revitalizing your congregation. There is plenty of room for growth in the percentage of our congregation that is involved in mission-shaped teams. Touch people where their interests lie. Find ways to bring together various people who share a common concern or vision. Allow them to develop their own way of being, sharing, living, praying, doing. As Paul reminds us, we do not need to be the same, for as a body has both eyes and ears, both a nose and a mouth, both hands and feet, so we as the body of Christ need to celebrate our variety of gifts, perspectives, and viewpoints. Successful congregations, congregations that are open to transformation, are congregations that honor the gifts of everyone. A small group ministry is one way to do just that.

Promptness Matters

Promptness does matter. People who are habitually late are viewed with irritation and even suspicion as though they are not trustworthy. When people give their word that they will be at a certain place at a certain time, it is not appropriate to unilaterally break that joint decision. Tardiness breaks trust. Consistently being late is a bad habit.

You can be on the way to transformational leadership by eliminating that habit easily, at least easily for most people. I smile as I say that, because I am thinking of someone that is so often late that if that person ever came on time, the whole group would wonder what had transformed the individual! It's about living in rhythm and taking time to breathe in a relaxed way, rather than panting from the stress of rushing.

Ed tells of the time his work schedule changed so that he had to drive during rush hour, and it was an anxiety he wanted to get rid of. One day he mentioned his irritation to a colleague, Dave, who simply said, "There are two things that helped me in my rush-hour driving; the first is using my rush hour driving for prayer, and the second is to stay in my own lane." Dave's wise advice changed Ed's focus. Dave simply replaced something he had in the category called "urgent" with something in the category called "important."

When I was young I used to be in a hurry to get places and developed the habit of speeding. One day a state patrolman pulled me over and commented, "I've been following you for five miles. I could tell the minute I saw you that you were somebody who was in a hurry. Is that the way you'd like to live?"

Being in a hurry is also disrespectful, isn't it? When we are habitually in a hurry, we are implying that our agenda and our priorities are more important than the other person's. When we take our time, we think more clearly, we do better work, and we often accomplish more in less time. We have both found that by taking our time we can create an atmosphere for transformation that makes it possible to do things more efficiently and therefore in less time.

Brevity Matters

Taking your time quickly refers to promptly trusting in God. We don't need to have the analysis paralysis. We don't need to hang on to things, even if there's a payoff waiting for us. That we can let go of everything that bothers us doesn't mean we sit idly by and wait. We have choices. That is central to transformational thinking. Very few congregation decisions could not have been made more quickly and briefly. We have all been held hostage by people who insist on talking a long time!

In November, 2006, SMITH magazine put out a challenge to its readers to offer a summary of their lives in six words. No more, no less. The invitation was spurred by a quote of Ernest Hemmingway, who mused: "For sale, baby shoes, never worn."

A lot can be said in six words. Try it. Some of the insights offered from the SMITH magazine invitation included such phrases as "afraid of everything; did it anyway" or "never really finished anything, except cake," or a phrase that could have a variety of implications: "not quite what I was planning." Try it—put your life story into six words. Reaching retirement, Bill sees a summary of his life as "worked too hard; played too little." We can say a lot about our priorities, activities, and personal pursuits in six words.

Jesus told stories about God and our relationship with God that were very brief. Yet did they not capture the essence of his message?[5] Jesus told several parables in just a few words: "The kingdom of heaven is like yeast that a woman took and mixed in with three measures of flour until all of it

5 Matthew chapter 13, has a number of parables that are very short; some are only one sentence long.

was leavened"[6] "The kingdom of heaven is like treasure hidden in a field, which someone found and hid; then in his joy he goes and sells all that he has and buys that field."[7] Or, "Again, the kingdom of heaven is like a merchant in search of fine pearls; on finding one pearl of great value, he went and sold all that he had and bought it."[8]

What Jesus stood for, taught, and lived is sometimes expressed in six words. "Jesus lived, loved, taught, healed, inspired." "Jesus showed us God and purpose." Texting and tweeting limits the amount of the content, but can enhance meaning by urging us to state what is truly essential. Using six words to deliver messages is not that different. It reminds us to focus on what is truly important. Why the early church used the symbol of the fish, from the Greek word "*ixthus*," as a way of communicating their faith. That word of five letters in Greek, stood for six words in English: "Jesus Christ, Son of God, Savior." Do we need more words to summarize all of the theological insight that has been contained in thousands and thousands of books since Jesus' time on earth?

A Relationship-Strengthening Exercise in Six Words

Recently I was at a wedding at which the presiding minister asked the couple to name six things they liked about their partner. What an imaginative way to offer a succinct, clear statement of one's love and commitment for another!

Some of us pastors have a propensity to use more words than necessary. Jesus could summarize centuries of teachings on the law into two lines: "Love the Lord your God, and love your neighbor as yourself." Do we need more than, "Love the Lord; love your neighbor"? Six words in total. Briefer can be more dynamic.

At a funeral last year the funeral director called me aside and said: "Those were beautiful words—what a tribute to the faith and life led by this woman. It was so powerful how you summarized the previous speakers and offered your own insights on the scriptures in a matter of a few lines."

6 Matthew 13:33.
7 Matthew 13:44.
8 Matthew 13:45.

Another funeral director standing nearby was blunter in expressing her affirmation: "Teach some of your colleagues 'less often is more.' Too many seem to think they must preach a lengthy sermon, even repeating the individual's key life moments after many speakers have offered their own tribute and memories of the deceased. It is as if nothing counts unless it comes from an ordained minister."

People come to a funeral or memorial service with their own memories, thoughts, and sense of loss related to the death of a loved one; they need time to grieve and to heal. They are looking for a comforting image or memory to get them through the next day, even the next week. They do not need to be bombarded by a lot of words. Today's preachers would benefit from using fewer words, not more.

Leave Room for Others' Spiritual Knitting

Many who come to worship come to do what the Rev. Dr. Malcom Sinclair called their spiritual knitting.[9] They may have concern, fear, uncertainty, personal crisis or loss that weighs heavily upon their hearts and souls. That is part of their reason for attending worship and it is wise for us worship leaders to leave room for that. When people have something they are working on, an effective preacher gives them some wool and maybe some new stitches to try, but the hard work is going on within the pews as the preacher does his or her thing at the front. Effective preachers could learn a lot from that image. Yes, indeed, sometimes fewer words from the preacher is the better choice.

People look for simplicity in message, in style, in words, in dress, in appearance and in buildings. Many congregations, as mentioned earlier, now use video screens and PowerPoint to project service elements. It helps people keep their heads up while singing, and allows most to see words projected that may be too small when on the printed page. Yet even here, we learn that filling screens with words defeats the purpose of the technology. Fewer words on a screen is ultimately the more effective way.

9 This metaphor does not focus on the components of thread and yarn, but focuses on the underlying meaning of the practical advice to "tend to your own knitting." Biblical truth is not only learned, it is applied.

And fewer words on the screen ultimately means more is expected of the people to offer in prayer (through silence), in worship (through sharing) or in the sermon (through dialogue). Gone are the days where people expect the minister to do the theological thinking for the congregation. Just the opposite is true; more and more people are looking for opportunities to engage in theological sharing and offering theological insight. That is why they become a part of a congregation, especially a mainline congregation. They want to engage in fruitful discussions that generally do not happen anywhere else in their lives.

This kind of participation is expected also in mission activity. Many congregations seek hands-on mission trips to other communities or even other countries in order for people to live their faith. Today, believers expect to do their share of pounding nails on a Habitat for Humanity building project, or pounding home their call to justice by writing letters to government officials at home and abroad.

Living and sharing our faith in Jesus Christ is too important to leave it up to others. We seek to get involved ourselves. Jesus calls all of us—not just our mind, or our soul or our spirit, or our body. Jesus calls our entire being into new life. That's transformational.

Take your time quickly. Promptly trust in God. Know where God is leading you—as an individual and as a congregation. Be open to new ways of sharing the gospel, and living your faith. That too is transformational. And it is God-pleasing.

FOR FURTHER DISCUSSION

1. What did you learn about transformational leadership from this chapter? What are the advantages and disadvantages of permission-giving leadership?
2. Name one thing you might be interested in learning to do with technology. Why do you think that might be important?
3. Leonard Sweet suggests that modern technological ways of communicating help build relationships. They connect us with a vast array of other people. Do you agree? How can your congregation use Twitter, Facebook, and other vehicles to enhance its ability to build relationships with the wider community?
4. What wake-up call would help you grow, with God's help, in living the abundant life?
5. Imagine how you might introduce permission-giving leadership to your congregation. How would you start? Where would you generate support? Who is still missing at the table?

9

Transformation includes Listening to New Ways to Live the Gospel

"I say to you who listen..."[1]

"Listen to his voice..."[2]

"Let the wise listen..."[3]

"My sheep listen to my voice..."[4]

"Everyone should be quick to listen, slow to speak..."[5]

"He who answers before listening—that is his folly and his shame."[6]

Learning to Listen

A farmer's harvest was so great that it exceeded his storage capacity. He built a bigger barn. He clearly listened to his own voice, based on his personal priorities. Big problem: he did not check out his idea with God. He made up his mind, "I've got good net worth, and I think I will retire. I'm going to take it easy." God had "breaking news" for him, "I've seen your doctor's report. Tonight is your last night."[7]

1 Luke 6:27–31.
2 Deuteronomy 30:20.
3 Proverbs 1:5.
4 John 10:27.
5 James 1:19.
6 Proverbs 18:13.
7 Luke 12: 16–21.

That news would put one's net worth into a different perspective, wouldn't it? However, the point of this story is not about money or wealth or net worth at all. It's about listening. And there is a basic flaw in most every presentation I have heard about listening. In fact, I can assure you that this chapter will reveal to the reader that I too have capitulated to this flaw.

Let me illustrate. Has anyone ever said to you, "You're not listening"? Actually, this is not an accurate statement. In order to make the statement accurate, it should add the words, "to me." We are listening all the time. Dream theorists tell us that we are even listening when we sleep. It's just that we're listening to so many things throughout our day that we never pause to think about to what or whom we are listening.

We listen to the TV programs, and we also listen to the commercials. We listen to our minds and also our bodies. We listen to all kinds of ideas. Sometimes we listen to those who are in need, and when we don't, it is because we are listening to something else.

And so it is not at all unusual for us to set aside certain specific times when we will listen to God. We will pray before meals. We go to church and listen for a message from God—at least for a little while. We read the Bible for a few minutes. The rest of the time we are listening to many other things, day and night. We cannot help but listen, for we are bombarded by all kinds of sounds, images, messages, and noises.

Most Always, We Listen to Our Ego

We could divide up the day into our workday and mealtime and rest and relaxation and leisure and growth, and we are basically listening to all the things that are going on around us, aren't we? Of course, we listen to God occasionally during our day.

At least we convince ourselves we are listening to God. It is more likely that we are listening to our "ego," which might stand for "Edging God Out." Simply put, ego is a failure to listen to God. Who is in charge? Who is the owner and who is the steward? Who is the master and who is the disciple? What is your goal in life and how do you find your purpose?

What Kind of Signals Does Your Ego Give You to Think About?

What kind of thoughts does your ego put in your mind to think about? Sometimes it seems as if some people are thinking about only one thing, most of the time. Though that's probably not accurate, I have found in my life that my thoughts were somewhat connected to my particular age. "When I was child, I thought as a child."[8] When I went to school, my thinking changed. When I got a job, I thought about different things. When I started dating, and even before that, I thought of other things. When I got married, I thought about still other things. Some of it has to do with maturity. "When I became a man, I put away childish things."[9] Some of it has to do with allowing our minds to be flooded by what we see as important, and not necessarily what God sees as important for us.

I have concluded that all of the things I thought about, even the nobler ideas, resided in the domain of my ego. My hunch is that people in the church are not all that different. When your congregation gathers as a community, or when your leadership team sits down for a planning and visioning exercise, do you seek out God's direction for your community, or do you get trapped pondering ideas that you bring to the process, unfiltered by the Spirit?

That, dear reader, is worth looking into. It explains, for example, why there is conflict in the church, or why congregation members are sensitive when hearing sermons about money, and even why we are resistant to change within our congregations. Ego.

Going back to the story of the farmer whose harvest exceeded his storage, we all agree that it is wise to put your money where it can't mold or rust, and that this is good stewardship. Yet accumulating a bigger net worth is foolish without a greater purpose, like glorifying God and building up the body of Christ.

But congregations are often adept at applying biblical principles to ego-centered, single-minded, overarching cultural principles around the subject of money. For example, congregations are regularly tempted to resist increasing their giving to missions so they can keep more

8 1 Corinthians 13:11.
9 Ibid.

for themselves. Have you ever heard it said within a meeting in your congregation (as if it upholds some basic gospel principle) "Charity begins at home"?

Many congregations have developed reserve or investment funds. Such funds, with extra capital investment possibilities, may assist in innovative ministries, new congregational initiatives, or provide funding to assist at a time of crisis and unexpected demands on the congregation's resources. Yet too often such funds are controlled as if the goal is to grow the assets without any regard to the ministry of the congregation. The congregation takes pride and joy in the size of the endowment funds rather than in the new ministries that they have initiated thanks to these assets.

One minister told us, "Our congregation has a 'rainy day' fund of $350,000. I am convinced we could be in the middle of a hurricane and our board would not realize that this is the very rainy day for which these funds were set aside. Why are some congregations afraid to spend money?"

Our assets as a congregation are given to us to share in the ministry of Christ, which is the way we seek to live God's mission on this earth. Having a bloated bank balance is never the means to live that ministry when a congregation is truly alive to the Spirit of God and reaching out to others.

I only use the subject of money as an example of egocentric thinking. Remember: Jesus was not one to wonder, "How much money have you saved?" Instead, he asked, "How much have you done for others?"

Many volumes have been written on numerous aspects of discipleship and wellness. We have many resources available in all areas of life enrichment —physical, financial, emotional, relational, and spiritual. I want to approach wellness and discipleship and stewardship through the lens of "listening."

Seeing Discipleship and Stewardship as a Lifestyle of Listening

Our bias is that transformational leadership revolves around effective listening. We are also biased that it is usually a myth when we think and even say that we are "good listeners." We are life-long learners. We get an education in order even to be considered for a position. We get on-the-job training. We practice job skills. This is true also for us with our faith practices. And we have a lot to learn about becoming good listeners, for it is not part of our normal educational processes. We celebrate those who speak well and articulate their ideas with eloquence. When was the last time that you heard it said of someone: "She is an outstanding listener"? Yet that is a skill probably even more important to our society, and within our congregations, than the ability to speak.

Have you received all the training to be a Jesus-follower? Showing up on Sunday morning for an hour is good and salutary—but it is not sufficient. Some denominations expect their followers to worship on Sunday morning, Sunday evening, and Wednesday evening. Our sisters and brothers in the Roman Catholic Church regularly attend mass, some of them daily. Followers of Jesus had worship scheduled every three hours, from Matins in the morning to Vespers before they went to bed. Our own worship "norms" are what we make them to be.

Training for discipleship for God is more than just showing up once a week (or once a month) at worship. It is a lifestyle of listening, listening to the right voices, listening to the right messages, listening with the intention of doing something about what we have heard.

Frankly, many of us have failed to read God's manual for life. Many of us have received little or no training about discipleship and stewardship of time, talent, and treasure. And when it comes to the importance of listening, we are woefully unaware. We have developed leaders who are good at telling us what to do and how to believe, but we have stopped listening for the still small voice of God. We think we have the answers, and that is how we structure our teaching.

Even some of the training we have received has been inaccurate or incomplete. Many critics have been very vocal about their concern that organized religion has corrupted discipleship. What began as a way of living, a way of being present for others, has become (in some presentations of the gospel) a way of developing an organization concerned mainly about its own survival. We have done that by telling people what to do. We have stopped listening, especially listening to God.

In this process of becoming self-centered, we have capitulated to our own opinions and biases and prejudices. Many of us have heard it said,

"I know what the Bible says about my salvation, but I find it difficult to see what it says about others outside of the faith." We have turned Jesus' teachings away from their original intent of being a net of hope for all, and have developed a hierarchy of goodness in which we are at or near the top, and others fall beneath our standards.

Do we know so much more now than people did in biblical times? In some ways we do. But this does not justify our reading the Bible with skeptical eyes, and insisting, "I know what the Bible says, but its message is dated..."[10]

We have confused ourselves by suggesting that the knowledge of our technological society somehow trumps the wisdom of the biblical witness. The wisdom of the Bible is never lost, no matter how much more technologically adept or scientifically aware we become in our day and age. The wisdom of the biblical witness is available to each of us in our congregational life. The Bible may not help us develop an energy efficient furnace for our sanctuaries; that is true. On the other hand, do you turn to your furnace to hear the wisdom of God shared in your community?

Unfortunately we know individuals—even individuals who offer leadership in congregations today—who have stubbornly made up their own minds and closed their ears to the teachings of Jesus and the wider community. In our cultural habits we accept that more is better—more money, more stuff, more assets, more opportunities, more choices. Why is that not the case when it comes to hearing the voice of God? Should not more understanding of how we can live God's mission bring energy to our congregations?

We still harbor the illusion that success is measured by what we have instead of who we are. We have become poor listeners generally, often not really listening to what others share with us, and that failure to listen is very evident when it comes to listening to the voice of God.

10 Matthew 15:9, Mark 7:7.

Scripture is Simple to Interpret, Yet Not Privately Interpreted Only

> *"There is nothing like the written Word of God for showing you the way of salvation through faith in Christ Jesus. Every part of Scripture is God-breathed and useful in one way or another—showing us truths, exposing our rebellion, correcting our mistakes, and training us to live God's way. Through the word, we are put together and shaped up for the tasks God has for us."*[11]

We have wrongly elevated our interpretation above God's own interpretation of God's Word, and have foolishly allowed ourselves to interpret the Bible according to our own biases and faulty human tendencies. Out of this morass we have come to believe such crazy notions as "Earthly wealth is ours," "It's our house, our land, our business, our congregation, our food, and our position." "It's my money and I want to decide how I will spend it!" The error is the words "my" and "our." Money is not ours. It is God's gift to us as a result of our God-given capacity. "Our" paycheck is something we earn only thanks to our God-given abilities. This notion of "our" stuff is patently false.

Recently Bill conducted the funeral of a community leader who lived by the motto: "Community service is the rent I pay for the privilege to live within this city I call home." Would it not be a very different process in our congregations if we started every discussion about future ministries and ongoing current activities with the affirmation: "Serving our community is the gift that God has given to us as we seek to share the gospel of Jesus Christ." What a powerful beginning for doing anything.

Such thinking counters the danger of coming to any situation with our own predetermined answers before we have listened to what God is trying to say to us. Who would enter an oral exam at university only to say to the presiding professor at the start: "Don't worry about asking your questions. I have all of the answers that you will want, so I will save us all time and just give you the answers now." Farfetched, is it not? Bill tells the story of showing up for a university exam that was announced to be an "open book"

11 2 Timothy 3:15–17, Eugene Peterson, *The Message*.

exam at a lecture he missed. He came to the exam and had no text to which he could refer. Very simply, he had no idea it was an "open book" exam. The exam was filled with quotations from the textbook, and the answers to the questions relied on a knowledge of where the quotations came from in the book. Fortunately Bill had thoroughly studied the material, but gave such evasive answers as: "I believe the quotation comes from the middle part of the book (chapter 4 or 5), and if I had the book, I could lift up other insights that the author shared to bring emphasis to this perspective."

Sounds odd, does it not? Yet some of us incorporate God into our lives in a similar way. "I know what God wants from me without ever questioning God or asking how God speaks to me through scripture, so I will just go ahead and do what I am supposed to do without questioning anything. I have a Bible but I do not need to read it, or even open it regularly." It makes as much sense as showing up for an "open book" exam without bringing the book. When we do not leave space to ask for God's guidance, we live as if God does not exist.

There is nothing in the world that is essentially ours, no matter what the property, deed, or mortgage document says. Everything belongs to God.

Everything Comes From God, With a Responsibility

Everything that God has given us is accompanied by a responsibility—to use all we have in ways that glorify God and build up the body of Christ. Yet we tend to hold on to "our" stuff tightly when we ought to hold onto it lightly. We store our valuables in a safety deposit box, which is fine for a legal document, but not for those things and gifts with which we could be making a difference in the lives of others. We have adopted the terrible skill of holding onto things with clenched fists. Fists that are clenched are symptoms of having hearts of stone. When our fists are clenched it is difficult to give. The good news is that the Holy Spirit crushes those hearts of stone.

Is Being 'Driven' a Good Thing or a Bad Thing?

It is true that we sometimes hear of people who accomplished great things because they were driven. But being driven is not usually regarded as a positive quality. We usually say a person is "driven" when we are speaking of someone who does things to excess. And even a blessing from God, when used in excess, becomes a curse. We commonly call it an addiction, meaning that we are incapable of using or doing something only in moderation. Even more serious is that it is also possible for people to drive other people to excess.

A book called, *What Do You Own and What Owns You?* makes the point that people may be driven by others or drive themselves to do something good for the wrong reason, or to excess. For example, money, in itself, is not bad; the *love* of money is "the root of all evil."[12] Our ownership addiction goes beyond money. In his book *God the Economist,* Douglas Meeks writes about the danger of what he refers to as the "white man keeper"—the individual who holds on to something in a possessive way, even when it is no longer of use to us, because we fear the emptiness we might experience in giving away our possessions. Yet we are called not to be controlled by our possessions, and if we have something we no longer need, the best thing to do with it is to give it away so someone else can use it.

In moving to northern Ontario, newly ordained, Bill and his then wife Ann, packed all of their possessions for the movers, saving the congregation considerable packing fees. They thought they had carefully packed the delicate dishes. They lived on the top floor of a three floor walk-up apartment building. The movers used a wheeled cart to take the boxes down the five flights of stairs to the front door, and as the cart dropped a step, a rattling "thump" could be heard. "Thump, thump, thump" went the contents of the boxes as the cart dropped from step to step to step.

Though well packed, all of the heirloom china dishes Ann inherited from her grandmother were broken. In pieces. Nothing salvageable. That was most unfortunate, but it was Ann's reaction to the damage that left Bill speechless. After her own initial shock and upset, Ann blurted out: "The good news is I thought I would spend the next fifty years of my life worrying about the safety of these dishes. I guess that worry just ended."

"That's it," Bill remembers saying to himself. A softy about legacy hand-me-down gifts himself (he only recently parted with dishes from his own mother and grandmother to help fill his younger daughter's china

12 1 Timothy 6:10.

cabinet), Bill could not believe the ease with which Ann let go of these special treasures.

Does your congregation hold on to the past so tightly you cannot move into the present, much less the future? Are you more concerned about how many plates were broken at a community dinner or glasses chipped in a recent celebration than you are about how the gospel brings life to your community? We adapt to changing circumstances and realities. Few measure the health of a congregation today based on the age of their dishes or the completeness of their cutlery set. Nor should they.

Many Can Influence Us, but True Motivation Comes from Within

We cannot motivate others without their openness to be transformed. Both motivation and energy are a function of desire. A proverb says, "A man convinced against his will is of the same opinion still." It doesn't motivate us to be forced to do something, or to participate in an activity because someone else said so. Certainly, intervention can lead us to have second thoughts and make some changes down the road, but we don't like to be pushed. We are more effective, and we are happier, when we motivate ourselves. The same is true of other people. They like to buy into an event, program, or opportunity of their own volition. We can make them aware of opportunities, but in the end we dare not judge them for the decision they make about whether to participate or not. There is nothing inherently wrong with waiting for someone else to motivate you. But what if they don't show up? Or what if we are not ready to respond when they do show up?

This makes it even more important that we listen to others in order to identify the areas in which the other person is already open to consider changing. One thing transformational leaders know is that, at a very deep level, one good idea will spark several more good ideas. If we listen to the insights of others, we will be nurtured ourselves into further awareness as we seek to develop new ideas and insights.

St. Ignatius says there are two things that motivate people—consolation and desolation. On the one hand, consolation, our dreams and desires can help create energy and power to build a better future. Sometimes opportunities are so powerful that they motivate us to do whatever is necessary to take advantage of the opportunity.

On the other hand, desolation means that our fears and difficulties also have power. Yes, "necessities are the mother of invention." "A teapot only whistles when it's up to its neck in hot water." However, some people are not consistently motivated by either consolation or desolation. In such cases, I suppose, we could pray for more hard times. My mentor told me, "Ed, it sounds to me like you're in a rut. If you are not inspired by what I have shared with you, I hope a wagon comes down your rut and jolts you into reality!"[13]

The twin transformational leadership principles here are, "Don't depend on other people to motivate you," and "Trust in God, and do something." God will provide, as Scripture assures us often, and we will not disappoint ourselves or others if we believe God is behind us and ready to guide our actions.

How to Help People Get Involved in Congregation Ministries

"But," you say, "people aren't always friendly, and I've had my feelings hurt a long time ago." Well, sometimes congregation leaders ask people to do the wrong thing; sometimes they ask people to do the right thing for the wrong reason; and sometimes they try to enlist others in the wrong way. You already know that hanging on to the past and not letting go of it just makes matters worse. Move on!

Congregation leaders often wonder, "Why don't people get involved?" "Why can't we get people to do anything?" "Why did they leave?"[14] They didn't get involved, they didn't do anything, and sometimes they left because of the way we treated them, or simply because they got involved in something else, and we have not bothered to find out. We thought we listened. We did not.

Consider instead adopting a new attitude, and then learn how to lead with a transformational leadership style. Our role in getting others to do

---

13 Jim Rohn.

14 David Kinnaman, *You Lost Me*, presents compelling evidence for many ways that organized religion has been insensitive, not only to guests but also to the entire generation of young adults who no longer participate in congregation ministries.

something in the congregation is not to sell them on it. We simply "sort and invite." Sort for specific gifts they have and sort to discern who has the best fit.

We also consider their personal style, their availability, and spiritual maturity, and also remain willing to invite folks who are not a perfect fit, because none of us is perfect. Just prioritize the best candidates to be future leaders. Pray in preparation before you invite them, offer them the opportunity to serve God, and then invite them to be in prayer to hear God's leading, and promise you will contact them in a few days. That's all.

Some of us will be willing to participate, and some won't. When will we stop asking for "volunteers?" That is an insult. Asking everyone to do something is also a waste of breath. Ministries are empowered and energized by people who have a passion, a calling to that ministry. Yes, lay people have their own calling, and we want to affirm their calling. Transformed congregations begin to wake up when they honor the call to ministry of all of their members. When we announce on the heading of the worship bulletin "Ministers: The whole people of God," we must be prepared to augment that statement by teaching the congregation what that ministry is all about, and then welcoming people to minister, so that the congregation truly does honor and celebrate the gifts of the whole people of God.

So begin new ministries with those who are willing! You find out who they are by sorting those who are ready from those who are not ready. Think back to your own experiences, and remember that there was a time you weren't as willing as you are today. Recall a time you didn't like being asked to do something you were not good at, and avoid making others feel the same way. And most of all, be patient with everyone. We only think of how patient others were with us was when they waited until we were ready.

Once you have a coalition of the willing, all you lack is a "champion" who emerges with a passion for that ministry. Sometimes you can find a champion first, and they will gladly assemble their own coalition of the willing. Some people wrongly criticize the reality that cliques do everything, and they don't like it. Let's stop calling them "cliques" and just say that they are small groups who have a common interest.

Replace Arm-Twisting and People-Pleasing with Respect

It is intrusive to arm twist, or try to make others feel guilty or afraid. The flipside is that it is hypocritical to pretend that everything is rosy in order to talk them into doing what you want them to do. If the shoe were on the other foot, you wouldn't like it either. It's not about trying to be a people pleaser. It's about being a people respecter.

Develop a passion for wanting them to be blessed by God, and then inviting them to develop a new relationship with God and the congregation. Do so in a cheerful way. Have enough of a relationship with them to know something they are good at doing. On occasion you may even find someone wants to learn a new skill.

When people give, they enjoy doing so because they were invited, and they get excited when they have a voice in how their gift will be used. We enlist gifts for many reasons. Invite people to give for the joy of giving. The root word for "cheerful" in the Bible is the Greek word *hilarion*, from which we get our word "hilarious." God loves a hilarious giver. Listen to another's heart and touch it. Listen to yourself and the words that you use, checking to see how you are coming across to the person. I confess that I regularly benefit from this reminder.

The United Church of Canada a couple of years ago changed the title of its unit that oversaw the financial development work of the denomination from "Financial Stewardship" to "Philanthropy." There was quite a lengthy debate around that change. Some felt that the traditional language of "stewardship," which has a rich biblical history and significant meaning to the vast majority of active people in the congregation, was being tossed aside. Balancing that perspective was a desire among others to use language that spoke to the community and members of today. Many understand the language of "philanthropy," as it has currency within our society. We hear about "philanthropists" who generously endow universities, hospitals, and community centers. Now we can speak about all kinds of givers—those who give relatively small gifts, and those who give considerable wealth—as philanthropists.

You Can Be a Philanthropist

What kind of giver are you?

One young man asked Bill at a weekend retreat: "If I give to the United Church's 'Philanthropy Unit' to help with the wider mission we do as a congregation, does that make me a 'philanthropist'?"

"I guess it does," replied Bill.

"I am so excited," came the retort from the young man. "I never thought I could be a philanthropist because I never expected to make enough money, and now I can be a philanthropist because I help with God's work."

We want to hold onto words that have had meaning in the past. However, new words may communicate better to a new generation of believers, and allow them to share their energy for the future ministry and vision of the congregation with excitement and commitment.

At another congregation at which he was a guest minister, Bill was introduced to a young couple that arrived with their baby. The minister whispered to Bill as they entered the church: "This couple had their baby baptized last Sunday. I am so glad they are back today."

The father of this couple asked how to go on PAR (a Pre-Authorized Remittance system that allows for monthly gifts to the congregation through automatic bank deductions). The minister of the congregation smiled and said: "You are in luck—the person in charge of the system is here today as our guest preacher. I'll introduce you to him."

Quickly I could see the young man tighten in his skin, worried he would be pressured into a commitment he could not make at this time. Suddenly he backtracked: "I cannot do much—I have a young child and work in construction that has been pretty slow lately. Since it is winter, my hours are very irregular. I cannot do much; on the other hand, I want to help the congregation on a regular basis."

"That is what PAR is designed for," Bill assured the young man. "The amount you give per month is your decision. No one will tell you what to give. That is between you, your wife, and God. The very act of seeking to make a regular commitment reflects your desire to be a regular and active part of this congregation. That is a special gift right there, and I thank you."

Make Worship Attractive to Guests and Inspirational For All

We sometimes mistakenly think that listening is something we do only with our ears. People actually listen with all of their senses, and with what we might call their sixth sense. People may or may not be concerned about what kind of clothes they should wear. But they are concerned about being comfortable. They wonder, "When do I sit and stand?" "Where are the restrooms?" "Am I welcome to participate in Holy Communion?" "How will this experience enrich my life?" Those of us who help lead worship can let them know that they will learn elements of the mystery of worship by participating. For the newcomer, the patterns and habits of worship can be confusing. Make the experience as understandable as possible for anyone who attends. If people have the tools to handle the small stuff of a congregation's worship experience, they then have the opportunity to be open to the larger presence of God.

At a congregation Bill formerly served, stoles were made and given to the children who helped lead the worship service each Sunday. When children participated in worship within the sanctuary, the one who did the readings wore the stole into the sanctuary, reminding all present that s/he was part of the leadership team. That's important.

Faith Listens for Opportunities to Serve

As congregational members, our faith is essential; it is a faith that is lived if we embrace opportunities to serve, and put our faith into action. It is often easier to feel things are going our way when we come committed, prepared, and willing to act and learn a task. A popular preacher on the airwaves recently preached a sermon entitled "Putting Action Behind Your Faith."[15] He stated that God is moved by our faith when it is lived openly and clearly.

Transformational leaders know that God empowers them and guides them—and they are willing participants in the transformation they seek.

Listening matters. Public speakers are aware before they begin their presentations that "Folks don't care how much you know, until they know how much you care." Knowing that, the good speaker listens to the

---

15 Joel Osteen, lead pastor of a mega-church, Houston, Texas.

audience before the audience even begins to listen to the speaker. And of course good preachers listen to their congregation in order to know the concerns bubbling up within the community.

Anyone can learn how to be a good listener. This is the path to effective communication. And effective communication is needed as we travel along the path to sharing the good news of Jesus Christ. Simply put, the road to evangelism begins with listening, not preaching.

How to Engage Guests Relationally

Suppose you meet a stranger in a casual setting. Do you feel comfortable starting a conversation? An easy way to start a conversation is simply to ask the other person questions about themselves. Start with general questions and move toward the specific. "How long have you lived here?" "Where did you move here from?" "What brought you here?" "Do you have family?"

Take your time. Ask as many questions as you can think of asking, in a gentle way. Feel free to share some of your own answers to the questions; just make sure your answers are brief and to the point. Then you can ask questions at the next level. "Do you have a pretty good idea how to find the services you are looking for in this area?" "Will you be looking for a church?" "What are some of the things your family might be looking for in a congregation?" "What kinds of experiences have you had in previous congregations?" "If you have any questions that I can help you with, will you please feel free to contact me either by my phone number or my email address on this card?" "I'm glad to have met you, and I look forward to getting to know you better."

My style is that I actually keep score of which answers to my questions indicate a hot button for the other person. And, my bias is that I "earn the right to invite." In other words, I am not going to make any overture toward the other person from my agenda until I identify three hot buttons of hers or his. Then I frame my response, beginning with a clarification whether I heard his three hot buttons correctly or not! Then and only then, do I frame my response. My response always begins with, "If there were a way..." for each of the hot buttons that he has confirmed as accurate, "... you would probably be interested in hearing more about it, wouldn't you?" In other words, the only way that I earn the right to invite is by listening and learning about the other person and any desires expressed to me in their search to live the abundant life.

That's transformational leadership, leadership that revolves around effective listening. And it's God-pleasing.

FOR FURTHER DISCUSSION

1. On a scale of 1 to 10, with 10 being the highest, how would you rate yourself as a listener? How do you think you can tell whether somebody is really listening? Do you usually check with the other person whether or not you heard them correctly?
2. What do you think causes hurt feelings? What have you found that works best for you in overcoming hurt feelings?
3. Do you find it appealing to say, "God loves a hilarious giver?" How does this speak to our understanding of "stewardship" or "philanthropy?"
4. Think of a friend or family member who is an exceptional listener. What makes them special? How have they encouraged you, by their example, to be a better listener?

10

Roadblocks to Transformational Leadership

"Here's what I want you to do, God helping you. Take your everyday, ordinary life—your sleeping, eating, going to work, and walking around life—and place it before God as an offering. Embracing what God does for you is the best thing that you can do for him. Don't become so well-adjusted to your culture that you fit into it without even thinking. Instead, fix your attention on God. You'll be changed from the inside out."[1]

This familiar Bible verse from Romans 12 is God's clear word. It is so simple that a five-year-old can understand it. It is also one of the most profound verses in the Scriptures. You can almost picture a motivational speaker getting us all excited, as though it is a spiritual vaccination, which, if we follow it we will be able to do everything we want to do. The Bible also says, "We are more than conquerors through Jesus Christ,"[2] doesn't it? Of course it does, and that is absolutely true. It's that simple. It is not a roadblock to transformational leadership. It is the path to transformational leadership.

What is the difference between a path to transformational leadership and a roadblock to transformational leadership? Roadblocks to transformational leadership are myths in disguise as truth. There is no such spiritual vaccination. Every day is filled with interruptions, temptations, difficult

1 Romans 12:1–2, Eugene Peterson, *The Message.*

2 Romans 8:37.

decisions, exhausting tasks, and ups and downs. As the cartoon *Peanuts* described it:

Frame 1: Charlie Brown says, "You win a few..."

Frame 2: Charlie Brown says, "You lose a few..."

Frame 3: Charlie thinks about it...

Frame 4: He says, "Gee that would be great."

Once and for all, let us expose the myth that all our good intentions can keep us from having bad days. Despite transformational leadership principles, our abundant life can be canceled out by any humanistic delusion.

This is so serious that if you swallow these myths, you will not have all good days and you will not avoid all bad days any more than you can avoid Monday by tearing the page out of the calendar. Ignoring any hindrance can ice your future, destroy your happiness, lead you into despair, and challenge the very faith that sustains you. Here are our nominations of the top ten myths that have deceived us.

Top Ten Myths About Transformational Leadership

Myth #10: "You can do anything you want to do." Many people believe this, but wanting something with all your heart does not make you able to do it. When I was young, more than anything I wanted to play professional sports; I wanted it with all my heart. Maybe some of you did too. I learned enthusiastically. I practiced with all my heart. Yet my enthusiasm did not transform my lack of talent. There are some benefits to having enthusiasm. But it takes more than enthusiasm to be a transformational leader. That's humanistic. The root word of enthusiasm is "in God." That's the only enthusiasm that is transformational. That's why it is true for us to say, "I can do all things through Christ who strengthens me."[3] And, "Be conformed by the renewing of your minds, which is in Christ Jesus."[4]

Myth #9: "You are what you think." If you think about riches, you will become rich.[5] That's what we'd like to believe. A best-selling book was

3 Philippians 4:13.

4 Romans 12:2.

5 Napoleon Hill, *Think and Grow Rich.*

entitled *As a Man Thinketh.*[6] The Bible says, "As he thinketh in his heart, so is he is... but his heart is not with thee."[7] The point of that verse, however, is that you can think you're on the right track, but may not be on it. Yes, if we don't bridle our negative thoughts, you're going to be negative. And yes, if you think positive thoughts you're going to be more positive. If you believe something with all your heart, you might be charismatic, but so was Hitler. He was the classic myth of humanistic delusion, the opposite of transformational leadership. "Whatsoever things are true, whatsoever things are honest, whatsoever things are just, whatsoever things are pure, whatsoever things are lovely, whatsoever things are of good report; if there be any virtue, and if there be any praise, think on these things."[8]

Myth #8: "Be all things to all people." This myth suggests that we should show different attitudes to different people in an effort to please everyone or avoid controversy. It is actually a humanistic distortion of a Bible verse in which St. Paul says, "to the weak I became as weak, that I might gain the weak: I am made all things to all people, so that I might by all means save some."[9] The Bible verse is true exactly as it stands, in Christ. That's transformational leadership.

Myth #7: "Buy now, pay later." This was the seductive temptation given to us by the credit card industry. The original advertisement promised, "Pay the easy way; use your credit card; it's the same as cash." The credit card was not the same as cash. We tried paying the easy way. But the bank wanted cash to pay for the credit card purchase. Credit is a humanistic nightmare that has no God-pleasing purpose. Scripture says, "The borrower is servant to the lender."[10] We need to instill a transformational understanding of the economic realities of burgeoning credit card debt. Sometimes we need to be saved from the world, and sometimes we need to be saved from our own missteps. Getting out of debt would be transformational for many families and, indeed, for many congregations.

---

6 James Allen, *As a Man (Person) Thinketh.*
7 Proverbs 23:7 (KJV).
8 Philippians 4:8.
9 1 Corinthians 9:22.
10 Proverbs 22:7.

Myth #6: "Get in on the ground floor." Have you heard that one? This myth is based on being part of the beginning of something, with the logical conclusion that if one is on the ground floor, one has no place to go but up. That is the myth. You can stay on the ground floor, and you can even fall into the basement. The expression got its start in US financial activity, as John S. Farmer showed by his 1889 definition of it in *Americanism*, "to be allowed to share in a speculation on the same terms as the original promoters." As we learn from experience, if the humanistic offer sounds "too good to be true," it probably is. Again, there's a wise Scriptural principle: "Test the spirits to see whether they are of God, because many false prophets are gone out into the world."[11] When we do our homework through the Holy Spirit, that's transformation.

Myth #5: "Have a finger in every pie, diversify." In our home I recall the violation of certain kitchen intruders who, before the meal was ready, could not resist testing every pie by sticking in a finger that they licked off. This myth refers more to being active in too many things, "jack of all trades and master of none," easily leading one to be overactive or overworked and ineffective. This concept also can be summed up by the term "busybodies." That's as close as a person can get to being anti-transformational. The author of the letter to Timothy said, "What you heard from me, keep as the pattern of sound teaching, with faith and love in Christ Jesus. Guard the good deposit that was entrusted to you—guarded with the help of the Holy Spirit who lives in us."[12] Good words for those who want to be transformational leaders.

Myth #4: "All's fair in love and war." Anything goes in this situation. The words appear in a seventeenth-century play *Love at a Venture* by Susanna Centlivre, and in an 1850 novel, *Frank Fairleigh* by Francis Edward Smedley. It also seems to be a model adopted in some sports in our day. "It's okay if you can get away with it." Very few things are as destructive, but we often find this destructive myth in congregations, especially those that are money driven. It is especially noticeable among congregations that take away offerings from the poor and the missionaries so that they

11 1 John 4:1.
12 2 Timothy 1:13–14.

themselves can have enough. This is just the opposite of transformational generosity that was characteristic of the Macedonian congregations; out of the most severe trial, their overflowing joy and their extreme poverty welled up in rich generosity. They gave as much as they were able, and even beyond their ability. Entirely on their own, they urgently pleaded with us for the privilege of sharing in this service to the saints. And they did not do as we expected, but they gave themselves first to the Lord, and then to us in keeping with God's will.[13]

Myth #3: "Go by the book." That means to act strictly according to the rules. There was a time when books with rules became widely available, but in Shakespeare, Juliet says to Romeo, "You kiss by the book." In other words, his kisses were not transformational. The myth of going by the book occurs when people take rules literally, to the letter. Going by the book is humanistic and legalistic. This is just the opposite of the verse that my father gave me when he helped us move our belongings to enter the seminary, "Not that we are competent in ourselves to claim anything for ourselves, but our competence comes from God. He has made us competent as ministers of a new covenant—not of the letter but of the Spirit; for the letter kills, but the Spirit gives life."[14] That was an unforgettable experience for me and it is a transformational verse that is engraved in my heart and inspires me every time I think of it.

Myth #2: "I am the master of my fate; I am the captain of my soul." This is about being in charge of one's own destiny and comes from a poem in 1888 by William Ernest Henley. Sir Francis Bacon said it also, as did Shakespeare and Tennyson. The idea goes back to Aristotle, "A man is the origin of his action." This is a humanism of the lowest order. It is self-righteousness, works righteousness. It is anti-grace. The only true transformation is that which occurs by the grace of God in Jesus Christ. Not just in our capacity to wake up every morning, but also for our promise of everlasting life. "For it is by grace you have been saved, through faith—and this is not from yourselves, it is the gift of God—not by works, so that no

13 2 Corinthians 8:2–5.
14 2 Corinthians 3:4–5.

one can boast."[15] We do not transform others. We cannot even transform ourselves. Transformational leadership is a gift of God.

Myth #1 about transformational leadership: "Make a 'To Do' List." This may be the worst roadblock. Daily "to do" lists delude us into thinking that we now have determined our priorities. Actually, just the opposite occurs. We have only made an "urgent list," which may or may not include any priorities. This is very important. The implication of the "to do" list is also sinister because it implies that anything that is not on the list doesn't need to get done. What is more, "to do" lists may leave one with the impression that something significant has taken place, whereas nothing has happened. All you have done is make a list. If you make "to do" lists, and use them to guide your actions, then I invite you to discover a way to transform those lists in this exercise.

How to Change Your "To Do" List Into a "Transformational List"

Do you know the game *Monopoly*? Few board games are found in homes today, but that is one game with appeal over the generations that may still rest in a cupboard somewhere. If you know the game, then you understand what I mean when I say that what follows is your "Get out of Jail" card. And you have permission to use it every day to stay out of the "To Do" jail. Please take out a sheet of paper and draw a line down the middle, and draw another line in the middle from side to side. You now have a sheet with four squares, or quadrants. Then label them:

Quadrant 1—Urgent and Important

Quadrant 2—Important but not Urgent

Quadrant 3—Urgent but not Important

Quadrant 4—Neither Urgent nor Important

Now list everything you want to do and put it in the quadrant that is most appropriate. If some of what you do occurs in more than one quadrant, list them in all of their appropriate quadrants.

15 Ephesians 2:8–9.

Now look over your sheet. Which quadrant do you think is most dangerous to your transformational leadership? The author of this theory says that the greatest danger to transformational living and leading is quadrant 1. That is the "Urgent and Important"[16] quadrant. A life lived there is a life that is dominated by a lack of choices. Living in "always urgent and important," subjects a person to a life of "tyranny."[17] It is a life that is completely out of rhythm and balance. Due to our own lack of foresight, or planning, or insight, we must respond to some kind of crisis every day while residing in that quadrant—maybe more than once a day. That is not transformational leadership. Transformational leadership makes quadrant 2 bigger than the others, and those are your true priorities. If this is one of the key principles that you have taken from this book, I promise you a life that is abundant. And it is God pleasing.

The roadblocks listed earlier are examples of spontaneity in excess, and this nullifies our capacity to set lasting priorities. Most of them are self-centered. None of them are transformational.

For example, "Buy now, pay later" has led to runaway debt and credit mismanagement. Unwise financial planning has ruined countless lives, and has kept people from becoming transformational leaders. Our experience is that congregations are now asking for guidance and training in God-pleasing financial planning, often because they have indulged in poor debt service. Many people whose lives are shackled with consumer-driven debt would benefit greatly from this area of transformation.

Debt Reduction is Transformational

Here is an excellent suggestion: Debt elimination begins with paying off the bills that could get to zero the soonest.[18] The debt elimination process speeds up dramatically when you can put additional money toward taking care of the other bills! A recent trend in congregations is a desire on the part of members to get help from their congregation in financial planning.

---

16 For a fuller description of this concept, read Stephen Covey, *The 7 Habits of Highly Effective People.*

17 Charles E. Hummel, T*he Tyranny of the Urgent.*

18 Dave Ramsey, Financial Peace University.

Vision planning often reveals simple improvements in congregation financial planning. While stewardship is more than money, it certainly is important for every member of the family and every leader of the congregation to live responsibly, and debt free. It is an important correction for one of the top ten myths that keep us from being transformational leaders.

Stop Blaming, and Make the Transformation Soil Fertile

Many people have a big problem with blaming others, especially in their early years. They simply pick up the habit of blaming others. It's almost as if they have a list of people to blame—the government, the economy, parents always making you do things, life being unfair, other people making more money, lousy neighbors who won't loan you any money....

We will give detailed guidance for eliminating blame in the next chapter.

Nobody wants to be a part of a congregation where there is irresponsible talk. That includes complaining. Here is a poem that has great transformational power potential.

The Grumble Family[19]

There's a family nobody likes to meet; they live over on Complaining Street,

In the city of Never-are-Satisfied; the river of Discontent beside.

They growl at that and this; no matter what happens there is something amiss.

And whether their station is high or humble, they're known by the name of Grumble.

The weather is always too hot or cold; summer and winter alike they scold.

Nothing goes right with the folks you meet, down on gloomy Complaining Street.

They growl at the rain and the sun; you can see their growling is never done.

19 Author unknown.

And if all went well there no doubt, they'd growl they had nothing to grumble about.

The strange thing is that not one of the same will acknowledge their family name.

For never a Grumbler will admit that he is connected with it at all you see.

And if anyone happens to stay, among them too long he will learn their ways.

And before he can think of the terrible jumble, he's adopted into the family of Grumble.

So it would be smart to keep our feet from wandering onto Complaining Street;

And not to complain, whatever we do, or we'll be mistaken for Grumblers too.

Let us live in contentment and song, even when things inevitably go wrong;

And whether our income is high or humble, we'll never belong to the family of Grumble.

Pharaoh finally agreed to let the Israelites go. You'd think they would be thankful, but they soon moaned and groaned and complained. They complained about the manna. They complained about the quail. They complained about their leaders. They complained that the good old days were so much better in Egypt. Finally, God simply said, "Complaining is not listed among the spiritual gifts that I have given you. I've had it with your complaining. Trip canceled." We hate change so much that even when we beg for new life, and seek personal salvation, we then complain when that new life is given to us because it means we must change.

Congregations open to transformation are willing to change; in fact, even the possibility for transformation demands that a congregation already has a significant number of people who are active change agents in order to instill a new mindset within the community of faith.

While there is no room for complainers within the gathered community, there also is no room for those who need to take credit for everything that happens. That particularly is true of leadership in a congregation. (Yes, ministry team, you are *not* exempt from this principle.)

The best way to have any good idea squandered and lost is to argue over whose idea it was in the first place. Better yet, think of the converse of this position: the best way for a leader to have a new idea adopted and implemented is to make sure it becomes someone else's idea. Here's how.

How Bill Handled a Congregational Need Transformationally

In 1981 Bill was interviewed in a small rural town to be the minister of a church with a congregation of almost four hundred members. As he approached the church building for the service that day, he could see that there was a major issue with accessibility. Over a dozen steps met the person trying to get into the building. That was daunting enough on a September morning, but almost impassible in winter since the community was nestled in a well-known snow belt in southwestern Ontario.

During the interview he mentioned the issue of accessibility, and asked if there were plans to make the church easier to enter, and possibly a clear intention to install an elevator to the sanctuary level. "We do not need an elevator; no disabled people come to our church." A succinct truism, since no disabled person could get anywhere near the entrance as it was then configured.

The vision of making the church accessible, and finding a way to install an elevator, never left Bill's mind, but he never pushed very hard, only offering ideas on how to improve use of the building that would include regularly pointing out issues around accessibility. When a member gave a substantial bequest at her death "for a special project," the beginning of a capital fund had arrived.

But even then, the issue of accessibility had not captured the imagination of the community as a whole, or even the key leaders. Only when the congregation's caretakers, a couple in their early thirties, mentioned the challenge of cleaning the church and hauling equipment from one level to another, and observing the difficulty some older members had in navigating the steps, did the interest in an elevator rise to the top.

A school bus garage next to the church came up for sale, and the purchase provided the additional property needed to complete the transition of the building. Bill knew the concept had a chance once it was someone else's idea, for then the community could latch onto the building program and collectively make it their own.

What Transformational Leaders Are Prepared to Do

Transformational leaders are those prepared to offer ideas, sit with them, and even encourage others to think in new ways, and have the patience to let the ideas resonate with the congregation and find their own time—really God's time—for completion. Transformational leaders do prod, challenge, inform, and they encourage the ultimate decision to emerge from the congregation. Patience is a quality that is necessary in a transformational leader. Transformational leaders also expose the myths that can so easily become roadblocks to transformational living, as we saw above.

One of the United Church's effective Stewardship leaders often said: "A minister can move into a congregation and make all kinds of change, then stay at least five or six years to help the congregation adjust to that change, or the minister may come in, assess the needs, plant seeds as to what changes may be helpful, then encourage the congregation in this new way of approaching their life and ministry so that change is implemented once the congregation is ready to embrace that change."[20] Both processes may take five to six years to fully implement and to elicit complete acceptance, but the latter approach of introducing change gradually may be less disruptive and more completely embraced, for the step of forcing chaos and unwelcomed disruption into the life of the congregation can be avoided.

Know your style and what works for you. Transformational leaders do not make change and run and hide; they are prepared to live and work with the congregation through the transition needed so that a new reality becomes part of the very fabric of the community of faith. Be a

---

20 In the 1970s and '80s, Craig Railton guided many congregations by reframing the lens through which congregations viewed bringing about change in life and ministry.

transformational leader who understands that for any group to be open to renewal, it must become a new being in Christ in order to live the gospel message for a new time.

Other Myths: Congregation Size, Delay, and Excuses

Just because a congregation or a company is big does not mean it cannot fail. Avoid even the slightest aroma of behavior that robs us of the transformational capacity that God gave us when he created us, redeemed us, and filled us with his Holy Spirit.

For example, postponing action can be dangerous. We generally do what is important to us. We delude ourselves into thinking that we don't have enough time. We know that there is no such thing as not having enough time. The remedy for feeling like we don't have enough time can be summed up in one word: "sorting." When we sort or prioritize anything, we differentiate between those things that are more important and those that are less important. The sooner we learn to sort, the sooner we will make progress. And the more relaxed we will be. And the more fulfilled we will become.

If we were to ask you, "How many hours a day do you have where you live?" we would quickly say, both in Canada and in the United States, "That's silly; we have approximately the same amount of hours every day—about twenty-four, give or take a few seconds." We cannot create more time in each day, but we can use the time available in each day in more efficient and God-centered ways.

When we sort, and discern God's design for our lives, our priorities take on a life of their own. And the rewards are indescribable. That's called taking responsibility. And it's God-pleasing.

When we become skilled at sorting the wheat from the chaff, good things happen. And they happen sooner rather than later. "Take no credit, place no blame" offers the correct starting point when we wake up. It is the correct starting point for individuals and for congregations.

Sometimes transformation begins by inviting a member or guest—any member or guest—to participate in any given ministry with the principle, "No blame, and no shame. Just do your best and God will provide."

Prioritizing is a daily necessity that cannot be ignored. Prioritizing is sorting. It seems simple, but there are myths and roadblocks that can distract us from priorities for expanding God's mission. Enjoy busting these myths and discovering transformational leadership. Avoid the danger of spending all of your time on the emerging urgent business of the congregation, and be clear about what are the important ministry activities of your congregation, and plan for opportunities that enhance that ministry, and allow your congregation to live God's mission in the world. It is called living the Gospel. It is being a follower of Jesus Christ. And, yes, it is God-pleasing.

FOR FURTHER DISCUSSION

1. Do you sometimes slip into complaining? How do you catch yourself? Have you ever been inspired by someone who complains all the time?
2. Which myth was most challenging for you? Why?
3. What distractions get in your way and lead you away from embracing transformational leadership? How do you handle them?
4. What suggestions do you find most helpful on your journey toward transformational leadership?
5. Do you function in your congregation on the basis of setting priorities or on the basis of responding to crises? What needs to change in your congregation to make sure God-given priorities are your focus in ministry?

CHAPTER 11

TRANSFORMATION WAKE-UP CALL TO EMBRACE CONFLICT

"Therefore, if anyone is in Christ, he is a new creation; the old has gone, the new has come! All this is from God, who reconciled us to himself through Christ and gave us the ministry of reconciliation: that God was reconciling the world to himself in Christ, not counting men's sins against them. And he has committed to us the message of reconciliation. We are therefore Christ's ambassadors, as though God were making his appeal through us. We implore you on Christ's behalf..."[1]

"Be conformed by the renewal of your minds in Christ Jesus."[2]

This may become your favorite chapter on the journey to congregation renewal. It is ours. It may also be the most important chapter.

We now address what could be the single most important controversial issue facing the church today. More controversial than any issue *du jour*. The most important cause for the decline of mainline congregations for over fifty years may not be doctrinal. It may not be over any interpretation of Scripture.

We probably agree that there may be numerous reasons for the decline of the church. But there is one correction that could make an immediate impact on the transformational functioning of the congregation. And if this is accurate, we could be much closer to being a healthy congregation

1 2 Corinthians 5:17–20a.

2 Romans 12:1–2.

than we realize. We want you to learn that conflicts are temporary detours on the journey to transformation.

Conflicts Create Opportunity

On a trip, it is not unusual to come across the sign that says "Road Closed: Take Detour." An immediate decision is called for, and even though we don't like the detour, we are willing to change our plans without calling a committee meeting.

Detours are likely on any trip. The bridge is out, or the road is under construction, or the flight was cancelled. If it would be beneficial, we could turn around and go home, or we might stay and do something spontaneous, or we might call a friend. Delaying the decision may be an option, but there is always a trade-off. And the trade-off could be costly.

So it is with conflict within the congregation. Conflict has created an opportunity, however undesirable, but nevertheless an opportunity to be addressed right on the spot. Options immediately surface. When we delay addressing the conflict, we might be choosing the most foolish option, as silly as sitting at a "Road Closed" sign until the road is repaired.

In many cases transformational leadership and conflict management not only address the issue, but also provide the very "bridge over troubled waters" that enables the congregation to move forward in mission.

Conflict management is the congregation detour that enables believers to arrive at their treasured destination sooner. And if the treasure is congregation renewal, that's pretty valuable. Wake up. Embrace the conflict. Listen to what the conflict tells you about what is important to your congregation members and guests. Conflict only happens when people have passion—always a strong, important quality within any organization, especially the congregation. Use that energy and passion for ministry and mission.

There are conflicts within families, between nations, within ourselves, and throughout the world. So it's no surprise that there is conflict in the congregation. But congregations and denominations are notoriously ill equipped to resolve systemic conflict. Granted that differences of thought about core values and ethical questions or theological doctrines require more than mere open expression in order for transformational thinking to occur. Obviously, this blocks the possibility of congregation renewal. Road Closed.

That is not to say that we need to resolve the conflict before we can experience transformation. It is to say that those are different processes. In some cases the conflict may be so severe that the community intervention comes before transformation will begin.

In our congregation we sometimes "stuff" our differences to avoid conflict, and we sometimes "attack" others. Sometimes it looks as though we're only trying to convert others to our point of view, but this may be an illusion.

We may be motivated by money. We often are. We may be motivated by control. We often are. However, and this is the vital point, when we are done stuffing and attacking, we think that we have resolved the conflict if both of us have the same position on an issue. This is an illusion. Trying to escape conflict simply postpones it and can lead to larger differences and even splitting the congregation. Quietly capitulating or stuffing what may be a God-given thought as though it helps to build a false sense o agreement in order to avoid conflict only plants seeds for a much bigger conflict somewhere down the road.

When congregation leaders and pastors are unwilling or unable to discern the relative importance of differences, they are likely to get stuck. Yet conflict can be managed in many ways, but it may be important to have a trained facilitator from outside the system in order to manage the conflict effectively. A transformational congregation does not hide disagreement and conflict. Such congregations think ahead so that conflict does not bubble up in self-destructive ways later.

Let's use the metaphor of a bank vault. What is the purpose of a bank vault? The majority of people might answer, "That's obvious. It is to keep others from stealing the treasure." But isn't it equally valid to suggest that the purpose of a bank vault is also to provide a way to access the treasure?

The bank vault not only protects a great treasure, but in fact provides access to the treasure to anyone who knows a series of numbers on a little dial. Whoever knows all the numbers of the code to enter the bank vault, in the right order, could access the treasure.

You might know all of the numbers, in the correct order, except the last number, and it won't do you any good. You cannot skip the last number without forfeiting your access to the treasure. You can't even get forgiveness for forgetting the last number.

The most important issue standing in the way of congregation renewal, and broader church renewal, is simple conflict management that would open the door to the treasure. If only we knew all the numbers in the right order.

It is inexcusable for a congregation to be inept at conflict management. This is our central wake-up call to the congregation. If we don't enthusiastically embrace this wake-up call, the future of any congregation will be at risk. Implicit in this is a toxic attitude, "If other people don't take responsibility for managing conflict-causing use of the tongue, why should I?"

Please do not think we are implicating only those who have "joined" the church. Becoming a church "member," or "going to church," does not mean that a person has adopted all of the habits and behaviors that reveal one to be a follower of Jesus. Everyone who is connected in any way with the congregation has an equal responsibility to challenge irresponsible talk.

Learning to Manage Conflict is a Wise Skill for Congregations to Discover

We all know that dealing with health symptoms effectively is directly related to early detection. This chapter provides some practical skills that will help congregations manage low-grade conflicts. Equally important is that these skills will also help congregations continue to grow after a trained facilitator has successfully managed high-grade conflict.

When we parents raised our children with parental support and correction, we sometimes foolishly thought that we corrected the problem through the use of authority and control. This did not necessarily resolve the issue, and may have contributed to greater conflict later on, because conflict was not properly managed.[3]

3 Matthew 18:6.

On the one hand, when we adults had grievances against each other, in marriage or on-the-job, or in a congregation, we simply did not initiate the proper steps to manage the conflict properly, especially in the congregation.[4]

On the other hand, if we discerned that someone else had a grievance against us, we did not initiate the proper steps to manage the conflict.[5] We had never learned those skills. Perhaps we never learned that, no matter "who started it," no matter what the source of the conflict, the initiative to seek a solution to the conflict was still required of us. Some people reading this still resist the idea, even though it is a clear mandate of God. Remember: "Blessed are the peacemakers."

In other words, if you have an issue with someone else, it's your move. On the other hand, if you hear that someone else has an issue with you, it's also your move. Either way, it's your move. We take responsibility for what we have done, or failed to do; and we take responsibility for our reactions to what others have done, or failed to do. If we want to be transformational leaders, the transformation starts with us. Some of us have tried to take the path of blame in order to succeed, but we all pretty much discovered that it doesn't work out all that well.

We can hold congregation leaders accountable for not learning how to address conflict effectively. That's fine, in one sense. But it misses the point of what it means to be a congregation. All who are affiliated in any way with the congregation, regardless of whether they are members or not, and regardless of whether the person is a priest, a Levite, or a Samaritan, each has a responsibility to take initiative toward conflict resolution.[6]

If the conflict is at work or at a party or at the grocery store, when a conversation leads to a person attacking others, we are responsible for not taking initiative. If we do not raise our hand and question the defamation of others, we are contributing to the deterioration of our culture, our nation, or our world, whether we are at work or in our congregation. If no one challenges, or stands up for another, we are complicit in the violation. If we know of a virus and do not initiate action, we are spreading the virus. The

4 Matthew 18:15–18.

5 Matthew 5:23–24.

6 Luke 10:30–37.

responsibility rests with each of us. Anyone, of any age, can calmly speak up in a group and object to what was said. It is that simple.

"Strong positions" are not threats. If we simply put the best construction on the person who is taking the strong position, it could be that it is his excuse for stubbornness or a lack of anger management. Or it could be that he just got bad news from the doctor, or has had a terrible tragedy in his life sometime in the recent past. We may never know what that is, but it is up to us, each one of us, to speak up. When one person speaks up, it can level out the whole playing field and create an atmosphere where every opinion competes on an equal footing. When any one person speaks up without the agenda of trying to convert the other, the culture also changes into a path to transformational leadership and a joyful journey to congregation renewal. Everyone on the journey helps each other manage any conflict-causing blame by reframing the conversation with a renewal-causing suggestion. It all begins by seeing each situation as offering an opportunity, and not immediately viewing whatever happens as a burden.

Does Our Way of Speaking Trigger Conflict or De-escalate it?

We choose to redirect every conversation whenever there is one specific way of speaking that triggers conflict. There are many such triggers, and all of them have deep-rooted causes, but it is our singular intent to grow in our awareness of the need for a red flag whenever a conversation shifts to blame. This is a universal trigger that often escalates conflict because blame can stimulate an explosion that can destroy a relationship, whether in a marriage or a business partnership or a friendship or a congregation. Transformational leaders know how to reframe the conversation because they recognize that the trigger itself is only a presenting issue that doesn't necessarily need to be addressed in order to right the relationship. Something much deeper is happening in such situations.

For us, it's helpful to distinguish between "inflammatory triggers" and "avoidance triggers." Inflammatory triggers are easy to spot. They sound like an attack, and have high energy. They tend to be more volatile. Avoidance triggers are more difficult to spot because they defuse the energy, are subtle, are equally dangerous because they are manipulative, however subconscious, and both extend the conflict. Avoidance triggers are noteworthy because often they lead to individuals clamming up, or remaining silent, or ending a conversation by changing the focus.

It is a mistake to respond to any trigger. It distracts us from the actual conversation. Triggers are intended to change the subject in order to distract others. To respond to a trigger only derails the conversation, and reduces any real opportunity to lead to transformational action.

Inflammatory Triggers

"S/he started it!" "You do the same thing!" "It's your fault that I..."

Siblings usually quarrel with each other. You as a parent or guardian do not want to get tricked into being arbiter. It does not matter who you think started it. When you say, "Clean up your room," and s/he says, "I didn't make the mess," that's beside the point, and does not deserve a response.

I was at a meal table with the parents of a six-month-old. The child threw food in every direction, no matter what the parents did. The grandfather calmly said to his son, "You don't want to lose this one." When we are afraid early on to confront those who are acting in difficult and inappropriate ways, we allow conflict to escalate. Wake-up calls require reframing the conversation, and where a conversation is not possible, reframe the context or atmosphere.

Parents cannot afford to allow a rebellious spirit to metastasize without opening the door for severe long-term consequences. It would be wise to nip that conflict in the bud. If a six-month-old gets by with it, you can guess what he will become when he is twenty-five and forty-five years old. Congregation leaders cannot afford to allow a rebellious spirit to metastasize either.

We have all learned that it is not sufficient to deal with issues logically. The issue is deeper than logic. It is spiritual. Conflict management is fundamental to every relationship. If we fail to face what challenges us, in our individual or our congregation's journey of faith, it is a mistake.

Wake-up calls develop spiritual maturity, and spiritual maturity is of primary importance in a community of faith. Transformation happens as we grow in spiritual maturity. Besides that, if left unchecked, the messes in our homes soon appear in our schools and shopping centers and congregations. The messes in our congregations appear in our communities.

The messes in our communities appear in our country. The messes in our country appear in the world.

Avoidance Triggers

"Pay no attention to him; he's like that;" "He is a good person;" "He will get over it."

There are many such statements, and the intent of the people who say them is not always praiseworthy. They think they are "putting the best construction on everything," as the eighth Commandment tells us, but their purpose in saying these things, which are patently inaccurate, is to distract the conversation from focusing on transformational action. How we discern the opportunity in those questions is a function of wisdom.

In North America, in each of our homes, we have wastebaskets, even though in some parts of the world there are almost no wastebaskets. We have some guidelines for emptying our wastebaskets. "Will you take the garbage out when you have a chance?" This is a lower-level question than "Can't you smell the garbage? It's starting to stink!" which is a question of emerging urgency and crisis. Everyone has to clean it up, not only those who made the mess in the first place. "Hello, this is the Health Department and we have received a complaint from your neighbors that your garbage might be a health hazard to the community." Messes escalate.

Six-month-old children can learn not to throw food. Four-year-olds can learn about stewardship. Kids can learn how to clean up their rooms. Adults can learn how to deal with differing job expectations. Congregations can learn how to manage systemic conflict. If they don't, communities and nations won't know how to manage conflict either.

Success and failure are both caused by the same process: a few little things done every day over a period of time. When someone says, "He'll outgrow it," a ready-made path to procrastination leads to a highway that escalates into conflict that requires intervention.

If we do not resolve conflicts in the home we will address them globally. That which cannot be resolved organically on the lowest level of conflict metastasizes into serious levels of conflict. Hiring someone else to pick up the garbage does not necessarily manage the conflict. In New York City in approximately 1955, the garbage workers went on strike. Within three days, what had been a routine practice escalated to the level of an emergency that required the mobilization of the National Guard. The higher the level of conflict, the more enforcement is required.

The training must begin at home. One reader of a newspaper advice column wrote in, "Dear Susie, My mother is always on my back, 'Pick up your clothes, clean up your room, and put everything where it belongs.' How can a kid handle parents like that?" Susie replied, "Pick up your clothes, clean up your room, and put everything where it belongs." Another wake-up call.

The same is true of congregations. If we ignore small struggles, if we ignore the concerns of members of the congregation, we may soon find ourselves in a major, conflicted situation. Transparent communication does more than keep people on board. It helps everyone understand, it builds morale, and it improves the Spirit-given unity of the congregation. It also allows people to offer their input before final decisions have been made.

God came to earth to help clean up everybody's messes, and he did, in Jesus Christ. Jesus redeemed us from all our messes, and wakes us through the Holy Spirit to have the capacity to clean up messes throughout the world. Jesus never backed off from the messes he encountered. He spoke to them, and even died for them. Jesus never avoided conflict; he faced it. His way is our way if we truly are to be his followers.

Congregations Can Be Transformed and Transform Others

God's good news enables congregations to wake up to the fact that they have been redeemed in Christ, and the Holy Spirit has given us the capacity to be reconciled, and to reconcile others from our messes and theirs. That is how congregations can be transformational and change the world. We do not limit ourselves to looking for someone to blame without being part of the solution at the same time. The blame game gets us nowhere in congregations.

Wake up. Cleaning up messes is part of our ministry. Embrace the task with courage. It is not in a small way that God has demonstrated his love for us. It is the example for us to follow. Congregations can make an immediate improvement the instant they put a moratorium on blame and start growing spiritually. Without spiritual growth the moratorium only deals with the presenting issue, and not the underlying causes.

The transformational skill of turning stories around and reframing them creates wake-up calls. Jesus did that[7] to expand our understanding and pre-empt worse conflict. When we reframe the conflicts in congregations in relation to mission, it is amazing what can occur.

Reframing Blame and Personal Attack in Your Congregation

Whenever someone blames the pastor or congregation leaders, it is a simple thing for any person to say, "I see it a little differently. I think our pastor is one of the best pastors I have known." Or, "I was on the council once, and ever since then I support leaders in their difficult work, even when I disagree with their decision." Or, "Our congregation leaders do so many things for the good of our neighborhood, our community, and our world. I'm grateful for our other congregation members." All of these are wake-up calls, but they are so gentle that we sometimes don't even recognize how transformational they are.

With no more breath than it takes to blow out a candle, we can make a significant difference by transforming blame. That allows us to carry on the conversation in a calm and mature manner. And the congregation pulls together, focused on God's mission, rather than being ripped apart by blame.

While chairing a negotiating committee for the local school board in the 1990s, Bill was threatened by upset citizens (during strike action by the teachers) who threw dead animals on his front lawn with scathing notes. One person (a medical doctor no less) called to declare that blood would be on the streets if the strike was not settled soon "and you [meaning Bill] will be responsible for it." Not sure what the caller meant, Bill immediately upped his life insurance by $300,000, fearing that if something happened to him the future well-being of his family could be severely compromised. Attacking people rather than attacking (or better yet, engaging) the argument or issue of disagreement is a worthless exercise.

7 Matthew 5:22–44 lists six examples of Jesus reframing, e.g., murder, adultery, divorce, swearing, vengeance, unconditional love. Cf. also Matthew 12:6, 36; 26:29; Romans 10:18–19.

Labor strife may be an extreme example of conflict, but too often congregations behave similarly when they allow bitter words as though they defend the Gospel. Remember that Jesus offers to us all a much bigger tent in which to live and move and have our being. Once we start using language that is vitriolic against fellow congregation members, we are lost as a community of faith. We have turned the quest for spiritual nurture into a political exercise of personal disparagement. We see every day in our news reports how much personal attacks now control our political process on both sides of our border—in the United States and in Canada. "Be a good citizen. All governments are under God. Insofar as there is peace and order, it's God's order. So live responsibly as a citizen. If you're irresponsible to the state, then you're irresponsible with God, and God will hold you responsible. Duly constituted authorities are only a threat if you're trying to get by with something. Decent citizens have nothing to fear. They act justly, and demand that those in authority also act justly. Do you want to be on good terms with the government? Be a responsible citizen and you'll get on just fine, the government working to your advantage."[8]

Your congregation also deserves respect. Dismissing the gifts of leaders, or refusing to respect those in authority creates a toxic environment. When we label others, dismiss the ideas of others, and routinely find fault in others, we create an environment in which more time is required to be spent in conflict resolution than in congregation renewal. Transformational leaders create an atmosphere of renewal and hope. They clearly communicate that they are not in charge, but that God is.

In a recent post on his Facebook page, comedian John Wing wrote, "I have made it a habit to listen to people with different political views than I have, because if we only listen to people with whom we agree, we will never grow." Transformational leaders look for growth by creating a climate that is open to a variety of opinions.

Bill had an exchange with a former Moderator of the United Church that humbly underlines this point. Ten years before he became the United Church Moderator, Bill Phipps and Bill Steadman were sitting at a meeting, listening to the debate unfold on a controversial issue. Steadman turned to

8 Romans 13:1–3, Eugene Peterson, *The Message.*

Phipps at one point and spoke about a particular member's calm demeanor and clarity whenever he entered into a discussion. Phipps never lost a beat as he replied: "You would think that he has great wisdom and insight, Steadman, because he thinks just like you."

Transformational leaders have learned from such experiences, and are careful not to listen only to those people with whom they agree, or with whom they have shared significant experiences. Your congregation will be vibrant and alive when you deliberately go out and encourage new leaders and diverse opinions within your community. One way to assure congregation renewal is to make sure you have a variety of perspectives and ideas reflected in the make-up of any team, task group, or working group in your congregation. A diversity of outlooks, opinions, backgrounds, and ideas only makes any organization—and especially your congregation—stronger and more vital.

When Not to Listen

It surprises some people to hear that there are times when we should not listen to others. We do not advocate silent listening. We advocate active listening, participatory listening.

However, we in the church should not listen to foolish questions and mean-spirited communication. The reason for this directive is explained in the following verse: "There are a lot of rebels there, full of loose, confusing, and deceiving talk. Those who were brought up religious and ought to know better are the worst. They've got to be shut up. They are disrupting entire families with their teaching... Get on them right away. Stop that diseased talk of make-believe, and made up rules."[9]

Engage Others' True Concerns

Do you have struggles over the style of worship in your congregation? Do some people feel that worship is staid and tired? Do others rue the day that drums and guitars replaced the organ or piano? Do some want a more contemporary feel while others look for the "old familiar" gospel hymns?

9 Titus 1:14–16, Eugene Peterson, *The Message*.

Debates can be healthy. The first place to deal with such concerns is on your worship planning team. Who serves in that capacity within your congregation? It is important that your worship team engage and represent the variety of viewpoints in the congregation, because then the worship experience can speak to all of your people.

People do not need to have everything go their way, but people want to be heard. That can only happen when we seek to have as many perspectives as possible represented on our major planning committees and teams within the congregation.

Worship is certainly a key component of any congregation, and in setting up a worship planning team, it is important to look for a balance of perspectives, and an expression of diverse expectations around the worship experience. Diversity can lead to two completely different services, and better to plan for such a move than to alienate large elements within the congregation without due process in planning by opting only to focus on one half of the congregation.

Enter into Study and Reflection

For many years congregations have seen the helpful growth opportunities of using small groups instead of committees and boards to discuss things like potential changes in worship. Many of these groups are developed through the common interests of people within the congregation. People may gather around an interest in knitting or quilting, or they may gather around an interest in model plane building or woodworking; they may gather due to an interest in gardening, or an interest in travel. The topics and interests that will help form a small interest group are only limited by the imagination and the ideas that participants can provide.

Along with such bond-forming groups, congregations might consider specific book study groups and even Bible study gatherings. There is a renewed thirst for seeking to understand the Word as presented in the biblical witness. There are fewer and fewer opportunities to engage in biblical reflection or discussion outside of what a congregation may offer. People appreciate opportunities to engage in biblical reflection with someone who has studied the Scriptures carefully and openly.

At his last pastoral charge, Bill was amazed when twenty-three people signed up for a Bible study on the parables, around the book *The Gospel in Parable* by John R. Donohue. After picking the book, he realized that Donohue presented a book rich in scholarship and probably more academically focused than what a group of lay people sought for an initial study. Still, he persevered. Even more amazing, people kept coming and joining. Five times he had to order extra books to meet the growing interest. The congregation even extended the study sessions beyond the initial seven weeks, finishing up the week before Christmas, so great was the appetite for learning.

Find a book—a novel, a movie script, a personal faith journey, a study of the Bible, a biography—that gives you the material to engage in questions of life, faith, truth, spirit, and community. People are yearning for opportunities to examine their faith in personal ways and within the community of faith. When you provide such opportunities, you will prepare the ground for transformational thinking within your congregation because people will already have begun a process of personal renewal, and will have elicited an awareness of the value of pondering their own faith journey.

Re-energizing May Mean Reframing

We have the capacity to reframe emotional statements and volatile outbursts. Conflict management begins here. By reframing a statement we simply mean that we invite others to look at why they feel the way they do about an issue or incident, and we often grow more than they do by listening to their narrative.

The transformational skill of turning issues around and reframing them is very effective. Jesus reframed the Old Testament understandings of divorce and murder, and gave them a transformational perspective. We don't usually think of that as being a way that Jesus handled some of the conflict with the Pharisees;[1] however, as for us, so for Jesus reframing expanded understanding and pre-empted conflict.

Attacking people instead of asking questions or seeking clarification creates mistrust. When we operate on the basis of trust we conclude that a person is not deliberately being difficult or aversive. We ask for clarification because something is amiss from our perspective, and we will set the record straight. We ask without judgment and without upset. Remember our first transformational principle, "Let go of everything that bothers you."

No phrase or sentence is going to magically change another person's perspective. At the same time, people in conflict often benefit greatly from someone who just listens to them a little bit. Many people are voiceless and powerless. While it's not enough just to listen to people without doing something to help them, sometimes the listening really helps.

There are many different levels of conflict, and many ways of intervening or collaborating to try and help manage the conflict. No one method works with all levels of conflict. In fact, some conflicts are simply impossible to resolve without separation. When one party has made up their mind that the other cannot do anything to resolve the conflict, though it should be a last resort, separation may be necessary.

In Conflict, Who Rules? The Majority or the Spirit of God?

The good news for congregations is that the Holy Spirit provides incredible conflict management skill and perspective for all of us. Congregations that are open to transformation do not use voting as a sledgehammer that can alienate us from each other. Instead of saying "That vote of ninety to ten gives us a mandate to act," we look at such results transformationally, and ponder the reality as, "We have ten percent of our congregation who are still not convinced that what we are planning is the right action for this time. How can we help explain our plans, and possibly modify our intentions, so that this ten percent will feel a vital part of the plan moving forward, and others will still be as enthusiastic as they are now?"

"Majority rule" is not transformational, and does not seek to understand the views and attitudes of minorities. When we seek consensus and unanimous (or near unanimous) commitment to any activity or project, we are operating from everyone's strength.

Some years ago, while Bill was serving in Sudbury, Ontario, a new mission statement was developed for the local judicatory, Sudbury Presbytery. The presentation of the new wording came after a very articulate and detailed explanation of what a mission statement is— a short, concise explanation of your reason for being, something you could explain to another person between floors on an elevator.

Then the committee presented its statement. It was over a half page in length, used for the most part traditional church language, and hardly seemed unique in any way. Who could remember this statement and share it with someone on an elevator? Bill pondered to himself.

The vote was taken, and the new statement passed 37–1. Bill was the only one to vote against it. So startled was the chairperson at his negative vote in the front row, she asked why he voted against it. (Not the usual process, and he felt somewhat put on the spot by the question.)

He rose to his feet, and carefully formulated a response. "I reluctantly voted against it," he began, "as I respect those who developed this statement, and the work that went into it. They have captured much of what we do as a presbytery, and so I thank them. I failed to see, as we were encouraged to ponder, how this statement was memorable, concise, and an easy way to share who we are to someone else on an elevator. It is simply too long by those criteria, and so I voted 'no.' "

To Bill's amazement, others piped up and said they also felt it was wordy, but had said nothing for fear of offending the people who created this draft. Before the discussion died down, the motion that had passed was reconsidered (and it required a two-thirds vote to pass the motion to reconsider, given the fact the presbytery had just approved the new statement), and then the mission statement was referred back to the drafting committee for further work. In the end, the mission statement that was approved now reads as follows: "Seeking justice, offering hope, celebrating faith." What a change! Concise, clear, accurate, memorable, and easily shared between floors in an elevator. Interestingly enough, it echoes an earlier discussion of summarizing our faith in only six words!

When the new statement was approved, Bill was thanked for forcing the original draft to be turned back and redrafted. "I take no credit for the end product," Bill replied. "I simply voted my conscience on a motion presented some weeks ago. The credit for this re-examination initially goes to the chairperson, for she wanted all of us to feel comfortable about the final statement, not just the majority, and secondly to the court as a whole, for only the perceptiveness of presbytery members that we wanted a chance to create a more meaningful statement for the presbytery allowed for this new result. Finally, let's give credit to the drafting committee members, who heard the concerns expressed and courageously changed their whole report to bring this concise final product to a vote."

Yes, there are times when something even better than "majority rule" guides our deliberations and decision making. Here is one example.

Early in my ministry I found out how deeply rooted is the concern to keep the building neat and clean. A new room had been built by parceling off part of the large Sunday school room upstairs. It now left the Sunday school short one classroom.

Some suggested the children simply crowd together—after all, there were barely sixty children in the Sunday school in a congregation that once had over a thousand using the same general space. Surely they can manage in tighter quarters. I argued, on behalf of the Christian Education committee, that the new board room was ideal for the grade six class. They were beginning to mature and would live up to the care of the room that was reasonably expected.

The debate went on: "What if they bring food into the room; who will clean up?" "What if they have drinks in there, even hot chocolate in winter, and it spills on the new carpet—who will fix that?" As the debate went on I found myself using my outside voice to offer an observation that remains true for me to this day. "There are things worse than a dirty board room," I began, having got the attention of those gathered wondering what that could be, "and that is a clean room because no one is there on Sundays."

The board reluctantly gave the children the room for use on a Sunday morning, and in two years no incidents of spills or leaving messes behind were reported. Coincidently, the senior minister and I spent forty-five minutes cleaning up the gymnasium after that same board meeting, the location where the board had met to discuss the wise use of space.

Another congregation used creative reframing of the criticism over children making a mess by spilling Kool-Aid in the church. The pastor gathered everyone into the fellowship room, the location of the concerns, and distributed a well written responsive prayer for all to participate in reading together. The title of the one-page document was "Celebrating the Stains." They turned a lemon into lemonade (pun intended.)

Many congregations caused conflict because they have not celebrated important events of the past. Honor the history; cherish significant moments in your collective existence; find ways to celebrate the congregation's anniversary. Then get on with being a community of faith that is forward looking—innovative in its thinking, and inclusive in its being.

A large congregation in a small community called a minister a few years ago–at least the search committee asked the congregation to call a certain minister after interviewing several candidates. On the eve of the vote, information came to light about the candidate that made many in the congregation uncomfortable about asking this individual to be the minister of their congregation. The vote did pass, however, with such a narrow margin that the minister, on hearing of the controversy, decided not to come after all.

The congregation wisely decided to enter into a search mode again, only after an intentional interim pastor helped them in their healing and visioning process. There was a danger that the pains from the past might only continue the cycle of uncertainty and confusion without time to reflect and heal.

Healing is only possible when we free ourselves from old habits and struggles, when we become unstuck, when we "Let Go and Let God." And part of that letting go is understanding what God expects from us. Commitment and action is a two-way street: we rely on God, and God guides and encourages us. It also helps prevent congregations from getting stuck.

Transformational leadership smooths out the rough places. A wise congregation acts as soon as it gets stuck. And it is God-pleasing.

FOR FURTHER DISCUSSION

1. On a scale of 1 to 10, with 10 being the highest, how would you rate your ability to deal with conflict? What works best for you?
2. What guiding principles does God give us to help us express our differences with our leaders and authorities, and help us to resolve them, in a way that unifies us to carry out God's mission here and now?
3. How is your approach to handling blame and personal attack helpful to you? At a congregation meeting, would you be able to respond, "I see things differently" or even assert when the discussion deteriorates into attacking people: "Let us address the issues before us and not attack other people"?
4. How do you suggest congregations address the issue of integrating children into your programs and ministries? Some people see children as a source of joy, energy, and new life. Others are concerned that they leave behind a mess, and make noise. What is your relationship with children? What is the commitment of your congregation to a children and/or youth ministry?
5. In Jesus' day, if a parent came to worship with an upset child, what do you think Jesus would have done?

CHAPTER 12

TRANSFORMATIONAL PRAYER

"This is how you should pray..."[1]

"The Lord God is near to us whenever we pray to him."[2]

"Pray for those who persecute you."[3]

Do you believe that prayer changes things? A congregation prayed about where God wanted them to worship and felt that God was answering their prayers when He led them to rent Sunday worship space from a tavern. The space was always available on Sunday mornings. The rent was reasonable. Some members felt like they might utilize the power of prayer to get people to turn away from drinking, and concluded the space was an answer to their prayers. They were excited about making a difference in the community. They became known as the "tavern congregation."

One night, the tavern burned down due to faulty electrical wiring. The word traveled fast. It was the lead story on the news. One news reporter said, "Did you hear about the tavern congregation burning down? Some say the tavern congregation was praying against the tavern." And everybody laughed.[4]

The police officers investigating the fire met with the pastor and leadership team, "It's been reported that you have been praying for the demise of the tavern. Are you responsible for the fire?" The leaders of the congregation voted 11 to 1, "We didn't have a thing to do with it!"

1 Matthew 6:5–9.
2 Deuteronomy 4:7.
3 Matthew 5:44.
4 Is it possible that a majority can be so blind as to not see a call to "wake-up?"

One member wondered out loud whether the congregation should credit God for answering their prayers! He challenged, "Don't we say we believe in the power of prayer?" He reasoned further, "And if people in the community hear about a faith that is this powerful, wouldn't all of them want to learn more about having such faith for themselves? The rest of that leadership team soon silenced the member for his risky comments.

That story brought to mind a similar one, of St. Paul's United Church in Sarnia, Ontario, which burned beyond repair in the 1960s. Two young fellows, too young to be charged with the crime of arson, were found to be the cause of that fire. In the 1980s, the minister of that congregation, the Rev. Ted Paw, remarked: "People wanted to string these young men up in a tree or burn their likeness in effigy when the fire happened; now we are considering the erection of a bronze statue in their honour." Always the jokester, Ted was alluding to the fact that as a result of the destruction of their church, the congregation, unlike many of their neighbours in the 1980s, was blessed with a relatively new structure in a more open design that allowed for multi-purpose activities within the sanctuary and the building as a whole. The fire was tragic, but it had prompted a whole new opportunity for the congregation. They had been transformed through the experience.

Transformational thinkers take whatever comes their way and find ways to see the hope and opportunity in the moment. Have too many lemons? Make lemonade. Transformational leaders do not seek consensus by being accusatory or judgmental of others; such leaders are realistic about the situation in which a congregations finds itself, and then seek ways to find new life to share with others.

Whenever I have a bunch of bananas on my kitchen counter that are overripe, I see the potential waste. My mother saw an opportunity to make loaves of banana bread to put into the freezer for future luncheons. She was a transformational thinker and did not know it.

We Distort Prayer in Many Ways

The story of the tavern church with which we began this chapter makes the point that people can distort prayer needs and results in any direction that suits them. We distort prayer in many ways. We can be quite creative in attributing something to prayer, while at the very same moment not noticing very many other clear answers to prayers. For example, "Did you hear about the man who prayed for patience, and God sent him a neighbor who threw beer cans into his backyard?"

Virtually everyone has heard about prayer, but few understand it. In a seemingly hopeless situation, people might say, "He doesn't have a prayer." Is that really accurate? Where do these distortions come from?

We often view prayer as part of our bargain with God. Perhaps you have heard some of the excuses such as, "If our faith is strong enough," or "If your commitment is clear enough..." then you will receive anything you seek in prayer. That is too self-centered.

Let's be perfectly clear about this, because it's one of the main misunderstandings about life in Christ. All forms of self-centeredness cancel prayer.[5] Disobedience cancels prayer.[6] Stubbornness, indifference, and neglect cancel prayer.[7]A self-centered life is always inconsiderate, and is not helpful for faithful people who are facing debilitating pain or challenging illnesses or prolonged unemployment.

Prayer might not be "seeking" God's presence but acknowledging and discerning that God is already with us when we ask the questions, and leading us to the answers we need. Any prayer which does not discern God's will is basically self-centered and such prayers are not acceptable.[8]

If we are truly seeking the guidance of God, we will be open to answers that we have not already thought about ourselves when we utter the prayers that we offer.

There is great need for prayer literacy in our congregations. This also means that there is a great opportunity for congregations to discover transformation through praying. Learning how God can transform individuals and congregations through prayer is basic to everything that goes on in a congregation, individual, and family. God's Word has some incredible promises to us that come through prayer.

---

5 James 4:3.

6 Deuteronomy 1:45, 1Samuel 14:37, 28:6.

7 Proverbs 1:28, 21:13, Zechariah 7:13.

8 Exodus 33:20, Deuteronomy 3:26, 2 Samuel 12:16, Ezekiel 20:3, 2 Corinthians 12:8.

Some Examples of Prayer Life: Martin Luther

Martin Luther was once asked, "How do you pray?"[9] Luther suggested that we begin our devotional discipline by focusing on a small portion of Scripture. Luther meditated on Scripture texts. His pattern was to ask four questions:

1. What in this text makes me thankful?
2. What challenges me to change, and leads me to repentance?
3. Which prayer concern do I have other than my own wishes?
4. What in this text causes me to take action?

"T.R.I.P." prayers: Daily Texts

Our family sometimes practices "T.R.I.P." prayer life. An annual booklet, *Daily Texts,*[10] offers one Old Testament verse, one New Testament verse, followed by a prayer. And we are encouraged to use four questions that form the acrostic T.R.I.P. as a metaphor for our life-long journey:

THANKS: What in this verse makes me thankful?

REGRET: What in this verse causes me regret?

INTERCESSION: What does this text lead me to ask?

PURPOSE: What does this text encourage me to do?

You could do it differently if you like. There is no single correct way to pray. For example, you may find the letter "R" is best seen as "What in this verse calls me to repentance?" What is ultimately important is to listen to what God is saying to us. We find it can be very helpful to focus on a scripture verse.

What We Say is Often Less Important Than How We Say It

Besides listening to what God is saying to us, I have learned that "prayer words" are less important than the spirit we bring. My family and I pray

9 Martin Luther, *A Simple Way to Pray for a Good Friend*, 1535.

10 Mount Caramel Ministries publishes *Daily Texts*, one verse per day from the Old Testament and the New Testament, followed by a prayer.

"rough drafts," using everyday language, and let the Holy Spirit make sense of them.[11] These words were this morning's rough draft:

> *"Thanks for living in our hearts, Lord. We are grateful to be able to pray to you anytime, even when we list our senseless struggles and self-centered requests. We have hope because you told us you live in us. We regret trying to do too much our way, without asking for your help. We welcome your comfort and strong forgiveness. Help us let go of everything that bothers us (especially...), and be with people that we know or have heard about (especially...) and meet their needs. Connect these prayers to what we can do to be your answers, for the sake of others and for Jesus' sake. Amen."*

Your prayer life and mine can be as private or public as the situation offers, whether we are alone, in a group, on the phone, or on a webinar. There is a beautiful verse that says, "When two of you get together on anything at all on earth and make a prayer of it, my father in heaven goes into action. And when two or three of you are together because of me, you can be sure that I'll be there."[12] Bill and I both have a habit of closing our phone conversations with prayer. Can the Holy Spirit be on a phone call? Of course. It might be more of a question of, "Can we be aware of when the Holy Spirit is with us?"

Jerry is a friend of mine who has a unique greeting. Whenever someone asks him, "Hi Jerry, how are you?" he answers, "I'm grateful."[13] I really liked that. So I adopted the reply too. We find it to be transformational for others, and also for ourselves.

When those two words "I'm grateful" accurately describe my faith at the moment, they witness God's presence and love. On the other hand, when I am not grateful at the moment, the words "I'm grateful" turn into a prayer.

---

11 Romans 8:26–28, "God's Spirit is right along-side, helping us along. If we don't know how or what to pray, it doesn't matter. He does our praying in and for us, making prayer out of our wordless sighs, our aching groans. He knows is far better than we know ourselves, knows our pregnant condition and keeps us present before God. That's why we can be so sure that every detail in our lives of love for God is worked into something good." Eugene Peterson, *The Message.*

12 Matthew 18:20–21.

13 A lifelong gift from a lifelong colleague, Jerry Hoffman.

A seminar leader on prayer once told us something very unusual, "Next time, for those who are interested, I will teach you how to get everything you pray for!" I didn't know how to take the comment. On the one hand, it got my attention, and on the other hand, I muttered, "Impossible; it's just a gimmick." It was not a gimmick. It was more like turning the whole concept of prayer upside down.

It would be more accurate to describe the seminar leader's claim as a fresh way of looking at prayer. It was not a "way to pray" or "what to say." The following week, the seminar leader opened his presentation with the statement, "The quickest way to be disappointed in your prayer life is to focus on what you lack and what you want. It is the world's most dangerous addiction." I had never heard it expressed that boldly. It also accomplished something else, namely, that it prepared my heart for what I was to hear.

He said, "Here is how to pray to get what you pray for every time. Write it down. It is not difficult." Then, with maximum pauses between words, he shared this wisdom, "Pray... for... what... you... already... have!"[14]

The United Church of Canada recently asked its committee on Theology to draft a Theology of Disability. Jesus was one who was aware of people who were on the margins. He saw wholeness already existing among those who were blind, lame, deaf, disfigured, or suffering from leprosy even before healing took place. Wholeness is not living a perfect life; wholeness is finding God's spirit present and alive for us even when we may be discouraged, or suffering, or (in the eyes of others) disabled.

God sees the wholeness in each one of us. It is incumbent upon our congregational members to see the wholeness in everyone with whom we worship.

When we pray for transformation in our congregations, we are not expecting that God will transform us from a dysfunctional, listless, confused, or lost bunch of followers of Jesus into a community of believers integrated by a common purpose and a strengthened faith. Our sense of purpose, and an enlivened faith, is present already. Transformation, when we are truly

14 This is such a simple statement that we can almost miss the point. Think it through. Be connected to gratitude. Notice what happens in your own perspective, when you pray for what you already have.

open to transformation, turns death into new life. Dead congregations, like dead birds, are those who are not open to transformation—they are simply dead.

Years ago Bill's daughter Mary came running home with a small bird in her hands. An older neighbour boy had told her: "This bird is frozen; take it home and have your mother or father run it under hot water, and it will come back to life."

This Mary did, galloping across our front lawn with panic and excitement all at once lodged in her breathless words. "Mommy, Daddy, come quick—this bird is frozen and needs to be warmed up. Run it under hot water and it will come back to life."

Now a four-year-old did not factor into this entreaty that it was summer, July to be exact, and the temperature was 82 degrees Fahrenheit at the time. We are not talking about Canada in winter. The bird was not frozen; it was dead. Judging by the condition of the feathers and the temperature of the body it has been dead for at least an hour or two. Carefully, Bill tried to explain that the bird was not frozen, but dead, and there was nothing else to be done for the bird but to bury it in a quiet, safe spot. It was like too many of our congregations—beyond transformation, because their needs had not been attended to for a very long time.

Why We are Passionate About Helping Congregations Wake Up

Unlike this bird, our congregations need not act as if they are dead. We are passionate about helping congregations to wake up because we believe that many congregations have simply lost their purpose.[15] It's that serious. But they aren't dead yet. Rather, such congregations are at risk of dying from a lack of care for the spiritual well-being of the community of faith. Such congregations need to wake up before they can be transformed.

Transformation happens when we are ready to change, and committed to acting in energetic and wholesome ways. We are alive, and we want to

15 What we call, "losing your purpose" is sometimes nearly invisible and insidious, an often gradual development in congregations. While it can be brought on by a crisis, it is more often noticeable in affluence and apathy. In fact, crisis often brings congregations together with energy to expand God's mission.

come to new life and be reborn. Is your congregation awake enough to accept this process?

I am reminded that prayer is "conversation of the heart with God," in which, as in any conversation, it is appropriate for us to listen as well as talk. It is appropriate to pray about our relationship with God with praise.

Does your congregation pray for its members? I do not mean say an intercessory prayer on a Sunday in worship, though that is a significant way to connect with others. I mean does it deliberately, consistently, and with single-minded purpose pray for those who are a part of your congregation?

At First United Church in Waterloo, there is a small prayer group that meets regularly to offer words of prayer for members of the congregation. They pray the names of the congregation so that at least once every year each person is remembered in prayer. Those facing personal loss, surgery, illness, uncertainty, sorrow, or personal challenges are lifted up in prayer as well at these regular gatherings. On the particular day of the year that they remember a person, the prayer group sends a note to that person in the congregation to say that they have remembered that person in prayer that day.

The responses to those notes, while unexpected and unsolicited, remind the prayer group of the value of prayer. Many times people have identified an experience that let them know even before the note was received that they were being held in prayer by the community.

Transformation may be the goal, but prayer is the answer.

The apostle Paul announced that he had learned the secret of life. He said, "I have learned to be content."[16] "Whatever my circumstances, I am just as happy with little as with much, with much as with little. I have found the secret for being happy, whether full or hungry, hands full or hands empty. Whatever I have, whatever I AM, I can make it through anything in the One who makes me who I am."[17] The world needs to know this secret, to simply "pray for what you already have."

When we begin with gratitude, we have a content spirit, and that is the fertile soil in which our prayers are answered, without fail. When we are content, we have discovered a secret of life in Christ.

16 Philippians 4:11.

17 Philippians 4:12–14, Eugene Peterson, *The Message*.

While intercessory prayer is appropriate for ourselves in times of need, the primary intent is that we pray for others in need. And of course, there is a time for us to make a commitment to become God's answer for all who are in need: to do something for those in need, with God's help.

The biblical basis for this principle is, "In *all* circumstances give thanks."[18] How inclusive. We can think gratitude, whatever our circumstances. God's Word is clear. The word is "all." There are no exceptions.

How do you think Paul developed his list of gifts of the Spirit?[19] He tried to encompass all that a congregation offers, all that God has created in detailing our giftedness as people. Gifts are too valuable to waste time arguing about a hierarchy of gifts. Paul reminds us that God did not look at gifts of the Spirit as a mixture of the "in" gifts and the "out" gifts. Gifts are simply that—gifts. They are examples of the Spirit alive in our community. They are ***all*** to be celebrated. They all reflect the glory of God. They all are valuable within the community of faith.

Thriving congregations welcome the gifts of all those who are part of the community of faith and do not judge which is the most or least valuable gift. All gifts can build up the body of Christ if we are willing to honour the gift and the giver.

Does God really expect us to be grateful all the time? Be thankful when things go bad? Be thankful when we are broke? Be thankful when we're suffering? Be thankful when a member of our family dies? Be thankful when we're about to die? "Yes" to all of the above!

I've learned an outlook about all areas of my life. I have discovered a direct correlation between being grateful and being generous. I've discovered a direct correlation between being grateful and being happy. And I've discovered a direct correlation between being grateful and being in harmony with God's design for my life. Quite simply, when I am grateful for what I have, I am even more ready to be transformed into something new. The same principle applies to our congregational life.

I've also found that when I am ungrateful, I am stingier, not even thinking about God, and I'm unhappy. The biblical injunction to give thanks "in

18 2 Thessalonians 5.18.

19 1 Corinthians chapters 12 and 13.

all things" opens up like clouds parting. It seems such a wise way to live, simply to be grateful. It seems as though I have less conflict, frustration, anxiety, and am less irritated by others when I am grateful.

Being grateful is transformational. God bless you in your discovery of the transformational life in Jesus Christ.

Being grateful is also transformational for your congregation. "Wake up, church!" There's a whole new life there waiting for us. God is waiting to give it to us, and when are hearts are ready, we can expect to receive it.

We hope that today you are more awake than you have been in the past. We hope that you are newly inspired to write the next chapter of your life, as well as inspired to help write the transformational future of your congregation, with God's help.

Today really is the first day of the rest of your life. A gentle wake-up call may be sufficient, but "I'm grateful" may be the appropriate response to every wake-up call, whether it is gentle or not.

And it is God-pleasing.

FOR FURTHER DISCUSSION

1. If the tavern congregation really believed that their prayers had influenced the burning of the tavern, would you have supported their decision? Why or why not?
2. Which of the listed distortions of prayer do you think is most dangerous? Why?
3. Do you believe that prayer can be such a powerful reality that a congregation can be transformed by God through our prayers?
4. Does your congregation have a ministry of praying for others on a regular basis? If not, how could you go about establishing such a ministry?
5. Are you able to say that you "give thanks in all circumstances"? How will you help your congregation to be grateful, to wake up and be transformed for the future, with God's help?

FOR FURTHER READING

Bass, Diana Butler and Stewart-Sicking, Joseph (ed). *From Nomads to Pilgrims: Stories from Practicing Congregations*. Herndon, Va.: The Alban Institute, 2006.

Christopher, J. Clif. *Not Your Parents' Offering Plate: A New Vision for Financial Stewardship*. Nashville: Abingdon Press, 2008.

_________. *Whose Offering Plate Is It?* Nashville: Abingdon Press, 2010.

Jackson, John. *Pastorpreneur: Outreach Beyond Business as Usual*. Nashville: Abingdon Press, 2009 (2nd printing).

Kinnaman, David. *You Lost Me: Why Young Christians Are Leaving Church*. Grand Rapids: Baker Books, 2011.

Kinkaid, Julie. *Overturning the Tables: Consumerism, Children and the Church*. Toronto: The United Church Publishing House, 2008

Lane, Charles. *Ask, Thank, Tell: Improving Stewardship Ministry in Your Congregation*. Minneapolis: Augsburg Fortress, 2006.

Law, Eric H.F. *Holy Currencies: 6 Blessings for Sustainable Missional Ministries*. St. Louis: Chalice Press, 2013.

Levan, Christopher. *Thanks Giving: Growing Generosity Among God's People*. Toronto: The United Church Publishing House, 2005.

Lyons, Gabe. *The Next Christians: Seven Ways You Can Live the Gospel and Restore the World*. Colorado Springs: Multinomah Books, 2010.

McNeal, Reggie. *The Present Future: Six Tough Questions for the Church*. San Francisco: Jossey-Bass, 2003.

Nessan, Craig L. *Beyond Maintenance to Mission: A Theology of Congregation.* Minneapolis: Augsburg Fortress, 2010.

Richardson, Ronald W. *Creating a Healthier Church: Family Systems Theory, Leadership, and Congregational Life.* Minneapolis: Augsburg Fortress, 1996.

Rouse, Rick and Van Gelder, Craig. *A Field Guide for the Missional Congregation: Embarking on a Journey of Transformation.* Minneapolis: Augsburg Fortress, 2008.

Schwartz, David J. *The Magic of Thinking Big.* New Revised Edition. New York: Cornerstone Library, 1981.

Sweet, Leonard. *Viral: How Social Networking is Poised to Ignite Renewal.* Colorado Springs: WaterBrook Press, 2012

Vallet, Ronald. *Congregations at the Crossroads: Remembering to be Households of God.* Grand Rapids: Wm. B. Eerdmans Publishing Company, 1998.

Volf, Miroslav. *Free of Charge: Giving and Forgiving in a Culture Stripped of Grace.* Grand Rapids: Zondervan, 2005.

ABOUT THE AUTHORS

ED KRUSE is the son of an American missionary to Brazil who served as mission developer in a Lutheran Church-Missouri Synod congregation and an ELCA congregation in West Virginia, and served as Lead Pastor in a large congregation in Iowa. All three congregations doubled in worship attendance during his tenure.

Ed earned a Doctor of Ministry from The Lutheran School of Theology in Chicago. He developed stewardship resources for the Central States Synod ELCA. He led the design of stewardship materials and leader development for all synods of the ELCA.

He co-authored this resource on congregation renewal out of the firm conviction, "Every congregation, small and large, can grow, with God's help." He has developed an approach that combines spiritual gifts, home and family, and conflict management as the Founder and President of HealthierChurch.org, a growing group of coaches who specialize in congregation renewal.

BILL STEADMAN is in The United Church of Canada and has a track record for growing congregations through excellence in stewardship. Currently serving as Interim Pastor in Kitchener, Ontario, he coaches congregations in the United States and Canada, mentoring pastors and training coaches in renewing congregations through HealthierChurch.org. He has been a regular presenter at the North American conference on Revitalizing Your Congregation.

Bill earned a Doctor of Ministry from McMaster Divinity School in Hamilton, Ontario. He is known for hymn writing, white gift dramas, excellence in administration, and liturgical creativity. He has provided guidance to hospitals, government boards, and denominational judicatories in governance, team-building, and communication.

He co-authored this book on transformational leadership out of his conviction that "when we share the gospel as our God-given passion" congregation growth occurs, especially in equipping the Uninvolved, Under-involved, and Uninvited in local congregations.

WWW.HEALITHERCHURH.ORG